Common Object Services Specification, Volume I

AT&T/NCR
BNR Europe Limited
Digital Equipment Corporation
Groupe Bull
Hewlett-Packard Company
HyperDesk Corporation
ICL PLC
International Business Machines Corporation
Itasca Systems, Inc.
Novell, Inc.
O2 Technology, SA
Object Design, Inc.
Objectivity, Inc.
Ontos, Inc.
Oracle Corporation
Persistence Software, Inc.
Servio Corporation
SunSoft, Inc.
Teknekron Software Systems, Inc.
Tivoli Systems, Inc.
Versant Object Technology Corporation

Revision 1.0
First Edition
March 1, 1994
Jon Siegel, Ph.D. (ed.)
OMG Document Number 94-1-1

WILEY-QED

JOHN WILEY & SONS, INC.

New York Chichester Brisbane Toronto Singapore

Copyright 1994 AT&T/NCR
Copyright 1994 Digital Equipment Corporation
Copyright 1994 BNR Europe Limited
Copyright 1994 Groupe Bull
Copyright 1994 Hewlett-Packard Company
Copyright 1994 HyperDesk Corporation
Copyright 1994 ICL PLC
Copyright 1994 International Business Machines Corporation
Copyright 1994 Itasca Systems, Inc.
Copyright 1994 Novell, Inc.
Copyright 1994 02 Technology
Copyright 1994 Object Design, Inc.
Copyright 1994 Objectivity, Inc.
Copyright 1994 Ontos, Inc.
Copyright 1994 Oracle Corporation
Copyright 1994 Persistence Software
Copyright 1994 Servio, Corp.
Copyright 1994 Sun Microsystems, Inc.
Copyright 1994 Teknekron Software Systems, Inc.
Copyright 1994 Tivoli Systems, Inc.
Copyright 1994 Versant Object Technology Corporation

The companies listed above have granted to the Object Management Group, Inc. (OMG) a nonexclusive, royalty-free, paid up, worldwide license to copy and distribute this document and to modify this document and distribute copies of the modified version.

Each of the copyright holders listed above has agreed that no person shall be deemed to have infringed the copyright, in the included material of any such copyright holder by reason of having used the specification set forth herein or having conformed any computer software to the specification.

NOTICE

The information contained in this document is subject to change without notice.

The material in this document details an Object Management Group specification in accordance with the license and notices set forth on this page. This document does not represent a commitment to implement any portion of this specification in any company's products.

WHILE THE INFORMATION IN THIS PUBLICATION IS BELIEVED TO BE ACCURATE, THE OBJECT MANAGEMENT GROUP AND THE COMPANIES LISTED ABOVE MAKE NO WARRANTY OF ANY KIND WITH REGARD TO THIS MATERIAL INCLUDING, BUT NOT LIMITED TO, THE IMPLIED WARRANTIES OF MERCHANTABILITY AND FITNESS FOR A PARTICULAR PURPOSE. The Object Management Group and the companies listed above shall not be liable for errors contained herein or for incidental or consequential damages in connection with the furnishing, performance or use of this material.

The copyright holders listed above acknowledge that the Object Management Group (acting itself or through its designees) is and shall at all times be the sole entity that may authorize developers, suppliers and sellers of computer software to use certification marks, trademarks or other special designations to indicate compliance with these materials.

This document contains information which is protected by copyright. All Rights Reserved. No part of this work covered by copyright hereon may be reproduced or used in any form or by any means--graphic, electronic, or mechanical, including photocopying, recording, taping, or information storage and retrieval systems--without permission of the copyright owner.

RESTRICTED RIGHTS LEGEND. Use, duplication, or disclosure by government is subject to restrictions as set forth in subdivision (c) (1) (ii) of the Right in Technical Data and Computer Software Clause at DFARS 252.227.7013

OMG® and Object Management are registered trademarks of the Object Management Group, Inc.
COSS is a trademark of the Object Management Group, Inc.

Library of Congress Cataloging-in-Publication Data
0471-07684-8

Printed in the United States of America
10 9 8 7 6 5 4 3 2 1

Table of Contents

List of Figures

List of Tables

Introduction 1

1.1 Cosubmitting Companies

The following companies submitted the specifications which were approved by the Object Management Group to become the Common Object Services Specification, Volume I:

AT&T/NCR
BNR Europe Limited
Digital Equipment Corporation
Groupe Bull
Hewlett-Packard Company
HyperDesk Corporation
ICL PLC
International Business Machines Corporation
Itasca Systems, Inc.
Novell, Inc.
O2 Technology, SA
Object Design, Inc.
Objectivity, Inc.
Ontos, Inc.
Oracle Corporation
Persistence Software, Inc.
Servio Corporation
SunSoft, Inc.
Teknekron Software Systems, Inc.
Tivoli Systems, Inc.
Versant Object Technology Corporation

1.2 Guide to the Specification

Volume I of the Common Object Services Specification is composed of five chapters:

1. **Introduction**
2. **General Design Principles**
3. **Naming Service Specification**
4. **Event Service Specification**
5. **Life Cycle Services Specification**

This chapter provides an overall introduction to the Specification and a summary of key features of each service. Chapter two provides an explanation of general design principles for all services. Following this, each service is described in its own chapter. The first section of each service chapter starts with an overview subsection, and includes subsections on Design Principles and Resolution of Technical Issues (raised in the Object Services Architecture, OMG TC Document 92.8.4).

The following items are addressed in the General Design Principles chapter rather than per service:

- Service Dependencies
- Relationship to CORBA
- Relationship to OMG Object Model
- Standards Conformance

1.3 Summary of Key Features

Naming Service

- The naming service provides the ability to *bind a name* to an object relative to a *naming context*. A naming context is an object that contains a set of name bindings in which each name is unique. To *resolve a name* is to determine the object associated with the name in a given context.
- Through the use of a very general model and dealing with names in their structural form, naming service implementations can be application specific or be based on a variety of naming systems currently available on system platforms.
- Graphs of naming contexts can be supported in a distributed, federated fashion. The scalable design allows the distributed, heterogeneous implementation and administration of names and name contexts.
- Because name component attribute values are not assigned or interpreted by the naming service, higher levels of software are not constrained in terms of policies about the use and management of attribute values.
- Through the use of a "names library," name manipulation is simplified and names can be made representation independent thus allowing their representation to evolve without requiring client changes.
- Application localization is facilitated by name syntax independence and the provision of a name "kind" attribute.

Event Service

- The event service provides basic capabilities that can be configured together in a very flexible and powerful manner. Asynchronous events (decoupled event suppliers and consumers), event "fan-in," notification "fan-out," and—through appropriate event channel implementations—reliable event delivery are supported.
- The event service design is scalable and is suitable for distributed environments. There is no requirement for a centralized server or dependency on any global service.
- The event service interfaces allow implementations that provide different qualities of service to satisfy different application requirements. In addition, the event service does not impose higher-level policies (e.g., specific event types) allowing great flexibility on how it is used in a given application environment.
- Both push and pull event delivery models are supported (i.e., consumers can either request events or be notified of events, whichever is needed to satisfy application requirements). There can be multiple consumers and multiple suppliers events.

- Suppliers can generate events without knowing the identities of the consumers. Conversely, consumers can receive events without knowing the identities of the suppliers.
- The event channel interface can be subtyped to support extended capabilities. The event consumer-supplier interfaces are symmetric, allowing the chaining of event channels, for example, to support various event filtering models. Event channels can be chained by third parties.
- Typed event channels extend basic event channels to support typed interaction.
- Because event suppliers, consumers and channels are objects, advantage can be taken of performance optimizations provided by ORB implementations for local and remote objects. No extension is required to CORBA.

Life Cycle Services

- The Life Cycle Services define services and conventions for creating, deleting, copying and moving objects. Because CORBA-based environments support *distributed* objects, life cycle services define services and conventions that allow clients to perform life cycle operations on objects in different locations.
- The client's model of creation is defined in terms of *factory* objects. A factory is an object that creates another object. Factories are *not* special objects. As with any object, factories have well-defined IDL interfaces and implementations in some programming language.
- The Life Cycle Services define an interface for a generic factory. This allows for the definition of standard creation services.
- The Life Cycle Services define a *LifeCycleObject* interface. This interface defines remove, copy and move operations.

General Design Principles 2

2.1 Service Design Principles

2.1.1 Build on CORBA Concepts

The service designs use and build on CORBA concepts:

- Separation of interface and implementation
- Object references are typed by interfaces
- Clients depend on interfaces, not implementations
- Use of multiple inheritance of interfaces
- Use of subtyping to extend, evolve and specialize functionality

Other related principles that our designs adhere to include:

- Assume good ORB and object services implementations

  Specifically, one assumes that CORBA-compliant ORB implementations can *and are* being built that support efficient local and remote access to "fine-grain" objects and have performance characteristics that place no major barriers to the pervasive use of distributed objects for virtually all service and application elements and entities.

- Do not build non-type properties into interfaces

A discussion and rationale for all the above was included in the HP-SunSoft response to the OMG Object Services RFI (OMG TC Document 92.2.10).

2.1.2 Basic, Flexible Services

The services are designed to do one thing well and are only as complicated as they need to be. Individual services are by themselves relatively simple yet they can, by virtue of their structuring as objects, be combined together in interesting and powerful ways.

For example, the event and life cycle services, plus a future relationship service, may play together to support graphs of objects. Object graphs commonly occur in the real world and must be supported in many applications. A functionally rich Folder compound object, for example, may be constructed using the life cycle, naming, events, and future relationship services as "building blocks."

2.1.3 Generic Services

Services are designed to be generic in that they do not depend on the type of the client object nor, in general, on the type of data passed in requests. For example, the event channel interfaces accept event data of any type. Clients of the service can dynamically determine the actual data type and handle it appropriately.

2.1.4 Allow Local and Remote Implementations

In general the services are structured as CORBA objects with IDL interfaces that can be accessed locally or remotely and which can have local library or remote server styles of implementations. This allows considerable flexibility as regards the location of participating objects. So, for example, if the performance requirements of a particular application dictate it, objects can be implemented to work with a Library Object Adapter that enables their execution in the same process as the client.

2.1.5 Quality of Service Is an Implementation Characteristic

Service interfaces are designed to allow a wide range of implementation approaches depending on the quality of service required in a particular environment. For example, in the event service, an event channel can be implemented to provide fast but unreliable delivery of events or slower but guaranteed delivery. However, the interfaces to the event channel are the same for all implementations and all clients. Because rules are not wired into a complex type hierarchy, developers can select particular implementations as building blocks and easily combine them with other components.

2.1.6 Objects Often Conspire in a Service

Services are typically decomposed into several distinct interfaces that provide different views for different kinds of clients of the service. For example, the event service is composed of *PushConsumer, PullSupplier* and *EventChannel* interfaces. This simplifies the way in which a particular client uses a service.

A particular service implementation can support the constituent interfaces as a single CORBA object or as a collection of distinct objects. This allows considerable implementation flexibility. A client of a service may use a different object reference to communicate with each distinct service function. Conceptually, these "internal" objects *conspire* to provide the complete service.

As an example, in the event service an event channel can provide both *PushConsumer* and *EventChannel* interfaces for use by different kinds of client. A particular client sends a request not to a single "event channel" object but to an object that implements either the *PushConsumer* and *EventChannel* interface. Hidden to all the clients, these objects interact to support the service.

The service designs also use distinct objects that implement specific service interfaces as the means to distinguish and coordinate different clients without relying on the existence of an object equality test or some special way of identifying clients. Using the event service again as an example, when an event consumer is connected with an event channel, a new object is created that supports the *PullSupplier* interface. An object reference to this object is returned to the event consumer which can then request events by invoking the appropriate operation on the new "supplier" object. Because each client uses a different object reference to interact with the event channel, the event channel can keep track of and manage multiple simultaneous clients. This is shown graphically in Figure 2-1.

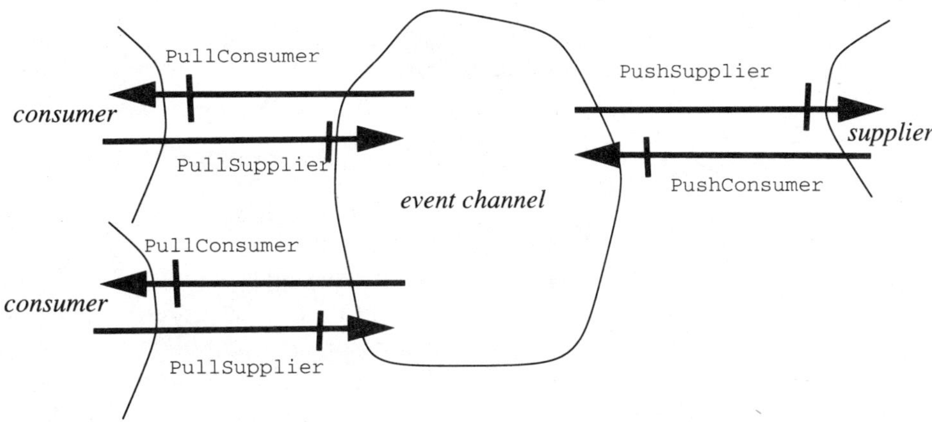

Figure 2-1 An event channel as a collection of objects conspiring to manage multiple simultaneous consumer clients

The graphical notation shown in Figure 2-1 is used throughout this document and in the full service specifications. An arrow with a vertical bar is used to show that the target object supports the interface named below the arrow and that clients holding an object reference to it of this type can invoke operations. In shorthand, one says that the object reference (held by the client) supports the interface. The arrow points from the client to the target (server) object.

A *blob* (misshapen circle) delineates a conspiracy of one or more objects. In other words, it corresponds to a conceptual object that may be composed of one or more CORBA objects that together provide some coordinated service to potentially multiple clients making requests using different object references.

2.1.7 Use of Callback Interfaces

Services often employ callback interfaces. Callback interfaces are interfaces that a client object is required to support to enable a service to *call back* to it to invoke some operation. The callback may be, for example, to pass back data asynchronously to a client.

Callback interfaces have two major benefits:

- They clearly define how a client object participates in a service
- They allow the use of the standard interface definition (IDL) and operation invocation (object reference) mechanisms

2.1.8 Assume No Global Identifier Spaces

Several services employ identifiers to label and distinguish various elements. The service designs do not assume or rely on any global identifier service or global id spaces in order to function. The scope of identifiers is always limited to some context. For example, in the naming service, the scope of names is the particular naming context object.

In the case where a service generates ids, clients can assume that an id is unique within its scope but should not make any other assumption.

2.1.9 Finding a Service Is Orthogonal to Using the Service

Finding a service is at a higher level and orthogonal to using a service. These services do not dictate a particular approach. They do not, for example, mandate that all services must be found via the naming service. Because services are structured as objects there does not need to be a special way of finding objects associated with services—general purpose finding services can be used. Solutions are anticipated to be application and policy specific.

2.2 Interface Style Consistency

2.2.1 Use of Exceptions and Return Codes

Throughout the services, exceptions are used exclusively for handling exceptional conditions such as error returns. Normal return codes are passed back via output parameters. An example of this is the use of a DONE return code to indicate iteration completion.

2.2.2 *Explicit versus Implicit Operations*

Operations are always explicit rather than implied (e.g., by a flag passed as a parameter value to some "umbrella" operation). In other words, there is always a distinct operation corresponding to each distinct function of a service.

2.2.3 *Use of Interface Inheritance*

Interface inheritance (subtyping) is used whenever one can imagine that client code should depend on less functionality than the full interface. Services are often partitioned into several unrelated interfaces when it is possible to partition the clients into different roles. For example, an administrative interface is often unrelated and distinct in the type system from the interface used by "normal" clients.

2.3 *Key Design Decisions*

2.3.1 *Naming Service Issues*

Distinct from property and trading services

Naming contexts have some similarity to property lists (i.e., lists of values associated with objects though not necessarily part of the object's state), and the naming service in general has elements in common with a trading service. However, following the "bauhaus" principle of keeping services as simple and as orthogonal as possible, these services have been kept distinct and are being addressed separately.

2.3.2 *Universal Object Identity*

These services do not require the concept of universal object identity.

2.3.3 *Life Cycle Dependencies on Future Services*

The life cycle specification describes the client's model of life cycle.

Life cycle move, copy, internalize, externalize and remove operations will need to accommodate graphs of distributed objects that are connected by *relationships*. Although not part of the life cycle specification presented here, an appendix describes a graph model supported by a relationship service to illustrate life cycle operations for graphs of distributed objects.

2.3.4 *Reliability, Performance, Scalability, and Portability*

These issues, identified in the Object Services RFP, are addressed in the chapter for each service, where necessary.

2.4 Accommodation of Future Object Services

The current set of interfaces may need to evolve in order to accommodate:

- Security (Access Control)
- Transactions
- Change Management (Versioning)
- Internationalization

In the case of the naming service, partial name resolution has been factored into the design in anticipation of security failures managed by a security service. The introduction of ACLs into the model should not effect existing clients of the naming service IDL interfaces.

The naming service interfaces may also need to be extended (e.g., the structure of names extended, additional name resolution operations added) in order to better support representing names and name resolution for some languages and/or cultures.

2.5 Service Dependencies

As shown graphically in Figure 2-2, the life cycle services interfaces are dependent on the naming service. The event service depends on no other service interface.

Figure 2-2 Service interface dependencies

The interface designs of all the services are general in nature and do not presume or require the existence of specific supporting software in order to implement them.

An implementation of the name service may use naming or directory services provided in a general-purpose networking environment. For example, an implementation may be based on the naming services provided by ONC or DCE. Such an implementation could provide enterprisewide naming services to both object-based and non-object-based clients. Object-based software would see such services through the use of NamingContext objects.

2.6 Relationship to CORBA

No CORBA extensions are required by any service.

The Object Life Cycle Service assumes CORBA implementations support object relocation.

Entities that are not CORBA objects—that is to say, not objects accessed via an ORB—are used for names (in the guise of pseudo-objects). In both cases the interfaces to these entities conform as closely as possible to IDL while satisfying the specific service design requirements, in order to enable maximum flexibility in the future. Specifically:

- In the naming service, name objects are *pseudo*-objects with interfaces defined in pseudo-IDL (PIDL). These objects look like CORBA objects but are specifically designed to be accessed using a programming language binding. This is done for reasons based on the expected usage of these objects.

2.7 Relationship to OMG Object Model

The specifications conform to the OMG Object Model. No additional components or profiles are required by any service.

2.8 Conformance to Existing Standards

In general, existing relevant standards do not have object-oriented interfaces nor are they structured in a form that is easily mapped to objects. These specifications have been influenced by existing standards, and services have been designed which minimize the difficulty of encapsulating supporting software. The naming service specification is believed to be compatible with X.500, DCE CDS and ONC NIS and NIS+.

These specifications are broadly conformant to emerging ISO/IEC/CCITT ODP standards:

- CCITT Draft Recommendations X.900, ISO/IEC 10746 Basic Reference Model for Open Distributed Computing
- ISO/IEC JTC1 SC21 WG7 N743 Working Document on Topic 9.1 - ODP Trader

Naming Service Specification 3

3.1 Service Description

3.1.1 Overview

A name-to-object association is called a *name binding*. A name binding is always defined relative to a *naming context*. A naming context is an object that contains a set of name bindings in which each name is unique. Different names can be bound to an object in the same or different contexts at the same time. There is no requirement, however, that all objects must be named.

To *resolve a name* is to determine the object associated with the name in a given context. To *bind a name* is to create a name binding in a given context. A name is always resolved relative to a context — there are no absolute names.

Because a context is like any other object, it can also be bound to a name in a naming context. Binding contexts in other contexts creates a *naming graph* — a directed graph with nodes and labeled edges where the nodes are contexts. A naming graph allows more complex names to reference an object. Given a context in a naming graph, a sequence of names can reference an object. This sequence of names (called a *compound name*) defines a path in the naming graph to navigate the resolution process. Figure 3-1 shows an example of a naming graph.

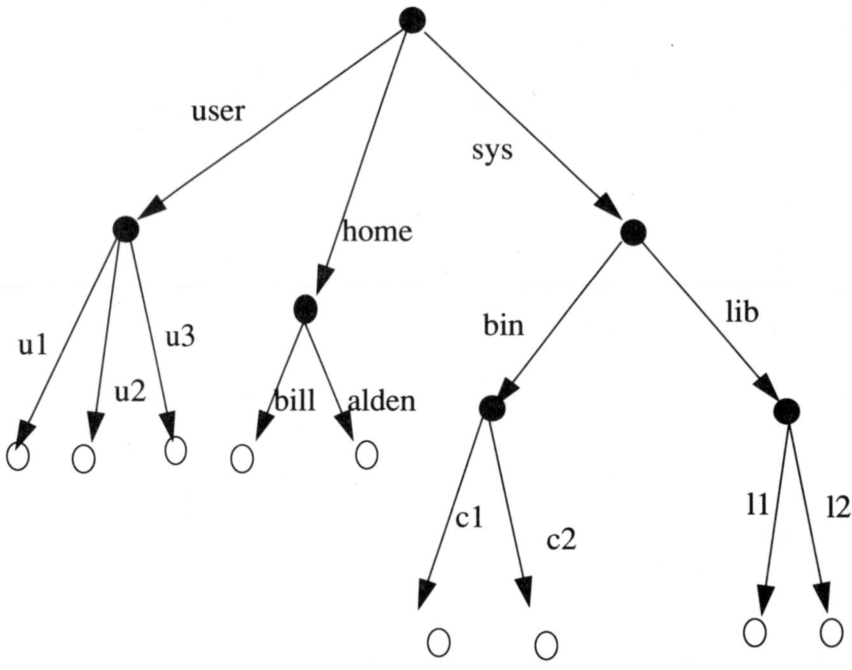

Figure 3-1 A naming graph

3.1.2 *Names*

Many of the operations defined on a naming context take names as parameters. Names have structure. A name is an ordered sequence of *components*.

A name with a single component is called a *simple name*; a name with multiple components is called a *compound name*. Each component except the last is used to name a context; the last component denotes the bound object. The notation:

```
< component1 ; component2 ; component3 >
```

indicates the sequences of components.

Note – The semicolon (;) characters are simply the notation used in this document and are not intended to imply that names are sequences of characters separated by semicolon.

A name component consists of two attributes: the *identifier attribute* and the *kind attribute*. Both the `identifier` attribute and the `kind` attribute are represented as IDL strings.

The `kind` attribute adds descriptive power to names in a syntax-independent way. Examples of the value of the `kind` attribute include *c_source, object_code, executable, postscript,* or *" "*. The naming system does not interpret, assign, or manage these values in any way. Higher levels of software may make policies about the use and management of these values. This feature addresses the needs of applications that use syntactic naming conventions to distinguish related objects. For example, Unix uses suffixes such as `.c` and `.o`. Applications (such as the C compiler) depend on these syntactic conventions to make name transformations (for example, to transform `foo.c` to `foo.o`).

The lack of name syntax is especially important when considering internationalization issues. Software that does not depend on the syntactic conventions for names does not have to be changed when it is localized for a natural language that has different syntactic conventions — unlike software that does depend on the syntactic conventions (which must be changed to adopt to new conventions).

To avoid issues of differing name syntax, the naming service always deals with names in their structural form (that is, there are no canonical syntaxes or distinguished meta characters). It is assumed that various programs and system services will map names from the representation into the structural form in a manner that is convenient to them.

3.1.3 Names Library

To allow the representation of names to evolve without affecting existing clients, it is desirable to hide the representation from client code. Ideally, names themselves would be IDL objects; however, names must be lightweight entities that can be very efficiently created and manipulated in memory and passed as parameters in requests by value. In order to simplify name manipulation and provide representation independence, names can be presented to programs through the *names library*. Note, however, it is not necessary to use the names library to use the basic operations of the naming service.

The names library implements names as *pseudo-objects*. A client makes calls on a pseudo-object in the same way it makes calls on an ordinary object. Library names are described in pseudo-IDL. The names library supports two pseudo-IDL interfaces: the *LNameComponent* interface and the *LName* interface. The *LNameComponent* interface defines the get and set operations associated with name component `identifier` and the `kind` attributes.The *LName* Interface includes operations for manipulating library name and library name component pseudo-objects and producing and translating a structure that can be passed as a parameter to a normal object request.

3.1.4 Example Scenarios

This section provides two short scenarios that illustrate how the naming service specification can be used by two fairly different kinds of systems—systems that differ in the kind of implementations used to build the naming service and that differ in models of how clients might use the naming service in conjunction with other object services to locate objects.

In one system, the naming service is implemented using an underlying enterprisewide naming server such as DCE CDS. The naming service is used to construct large, enterprisewide naming graphs where NamingContexts model "directories" or "folders" and other names identify "document" or "file" kinds of objects. In other words, the naming service is used as the backbone of an enterprisewide filing system. In such as system, non-object-based access to the naming service may well be as commonplace as object-based access to the naming service. For example, the name of an object might be presented to the DCE directory service as a null-terminated ASCII string such as "/.../DME/nls/moa-1/ID-1".

The naming service provides the principal mechanism through which most clients of an ORB-based system locate objects that they intend to use (make requests on). Given an initial naming context, clients navigate naming contexts retrieving lists of the names bound to that context. In conjunction with properties and security services, clients look for objects with certain "externally visible" characteristics, for example, for objects with recognized names or objects with a certain time-last-modified (all subject to security considerations). All objects used in such a scheme register their externally visible characteristics with other services (a name service, a property service, and so on).

Conventions are employed in such a scheme that meaningfully partition the name space. For example, individuals are assigned naming contexts for personal use, groups of individuals may be assigned shared naming contexts while other contexts are organized in a public section of the naming graph. Similarly, conventions are used to identify contexts that list the names of services that are available in the system (e.g., that locate the translation service, the printing service).

In an alternative system, the naming service can be used in a more limited role and can have a less sophisticated implementation. In this model, naming contexts represent the types and locations of services that are available in the system and a much shallower naming graph is employed. For example, the naming service is used to register the object references of a mail service, an information service, a filing service.

Given a handful of references to "root objects" obtained from the naming service, a client uses relationship and query services to locate objects contained in or managed by the services registered with the naming service. In such a system, the naming service is used sparingly and instead clients rely on other services such as query services to navigate through large collections of objects. Also, objects in this scheme rarely register "external characteristics" with another service—instead they support the interfaces of query or relationship services.

Of course, nothing precludes the naming service presented here from being used to provide both models of use at the same time. These two scenarios demonstrate how this specification is suitable for use in two fairly different kinds of systems with potentially quite different kinds of implementations. The service provides a basic building block on which higher-level services impose the conventions and semantics which determine how frameworks of application and facilities objects locate other objects.

3.1.5 Design Principles

Several principles have driven the design of the naming service:

1. The design imparts no semantics or interpretation of the names themselves; this is up to higher-level software. The naming service provides only a structural convention for names (e.g., compound names).
2. The design supports distributed, heterogeneous implementation and administration of names and name contexts.
3. Names are structures, not just character strings. A `struct` is necessary to avoid encoding information syntactically in the name string (e.g., separating the human-meaningful name and its type with a ".", and the type and version with a "!"), which is a bad idea with respect to the generality, extensibility, and internationalization of the name service. The structure defined here includes a human-chosen string plus a kind field.
4. Naming service clients need not be aware of the physical site of name servers in a distributed environment, or which server interprets what portion of a compound name, or of the way that servers are implemented.
5. The naming service is a fundamental object service, with no dependencies on other interfaces.
6. Name contexts of arbitrary and unknown implementation may be utilized together as nested graphs of nodes that cooperate in resolving names for a client. No "universal" root is needed for a name hierarchy.
7. Existing name and directory services employed in different network computing environments can be transparently encapsulated using name contexts. All of the above features contribute to making this possible.
8. The design does not address name security since there is currently no OMG security model. The naming service can be evolved to provide name security when an object security service is standardized.
9. The design does not address namespace administration. It is the responsibility of higher-level software to administer the namespace.

3.1.6 Resolution of Technical Issues

This specification addresses the issues identified for name services in the OMG *Object Services Architecture* document[1] as follows:

1. *Object Services Architecture*, Document Number 92-8-4, Object Managment Group, Framingham, MA, 1992.

- *Naming standards*: Encapsulation of existing naming standards and protocols is allowed using naming contexts. Transparent encapsulation is made possible by the design features outlined above.
- *Federation of namespaces*: The specification supports distributed federation of namespaces; no assumptions are made about centralized or universal functions. Namespaces may be nested in a graph in any fashion, independent of the implementation of each namespace. There need be no distinguished root context, and existing graphs may be joined at any point.
- *Scope of names*: Name contexts define name scope. Names must be unique within a context. Objects may have multiple names, and may exist in multiple name contexts. Name contexts may be named objects nested within another name context, and cycles are permitted. The name itself is not a full-fledged ORB object, but does support structure, so it may have multiple components. No requirements are placed on naming conventions, in order to support a wide variety of conventions and existing standards.
- *Operations*: The specification supports bind, unbind, lookup, and sequence operations on a name context. It does not support a rename operation, because we do not see how to implement this correctly in a distributed environment without transactions.

3.2 The CosNaming Module

Names of all IDC modules which form the Common Object Services Specification are prefixed with the initials "Cos."

The CosNaming module is a collection of interfaces that together define the naming service. This module contains two interfaces:

- The *NamingContext* Interface
- The *BindingIterator* Interface

This section describes these interfaces and their operations in detail.

The CosNaming Module is shown in Figure 3-2. Note that `Istring` is a placeholder for a future IDL internationalized string data type.

```
module CosNaming
{
    typedef string Istring;
    struct NameComponent {
        Istring id;
        Istring kind;
    };
```

Figure 3-2 The `CosNaming` module

```
typedef sequence <NameComponent> Name;

enum BindingType {nobject, ncontext};

struct Binding {
    Name binding_name;
    BindingType binding_type;
};

typedef sequence <Binding> BindingList;


interface BindingIterator;

interface NamingContext {

    enum NotFoundReason { missing_node, not_context, not_object};

    exception NotFound {
            NotFoundReason why;
            Name rest_of_name;
    };

    exception CannotProceed {
            NamingContext cxt;
            Name rest_of_name;
    };

    exception InvalidName{};
    exception AlreadyBound {};
    exception NotEmpty{};

    void bind(in Name n, in Object obj)
         raises(NotFound, CannotProceed, InvalidName, AlreadyBound);
    void rebind(in Name n, in Object obj)
         raises(NotFound, CannotProceed, InvalidName);
    void bind_context(in Name n, in NamingContext nc)
         raises(NotFound, CannotProceed, InvalidName, AlreadyBound);
    void rebind_context(in Name n, in NamingContext nc)
         raises(NotFound, CannotProceed, InvalidName);
    Object resolve (in Name n)
         raises(NotFound, CannotProceed, InvalidName);
    void unbind(in Name n)
         raises(NotFound, CannotProceed, InvalidName);
    NamingContext new_context();
    NamingContext bind_new_context(in Name n)
         raises(NotFound, AlreadyBound, CannotProceed, InvalidName);
    void destroy( )
         raises(NotEmpty);
    void list (in unsigned long how_many,
                out BindingList bl, out BindingIterator bi);
```

Figure 3-2 The `CosNaming` **module** *(continued)*

```
    };

    interface BindingIterator {
        boolean next_one(out Binding b);
        boolean next_n(in unsigned long how_many,
                    out BindingList bl);
        void destroy();
    };
};
```

Figure 3-2 The `CosNaming` module *(continued)*

The following sections describe the operations of the *NamingContext* interface:

- binding objects
- name resolution
- unbinding
- creating naming contexts
- deleting contexts
- listing a naming context

3.2.1 Binding Objects

The binding operations name an object in a naming context. Once an object is bound, it can be found with the `resolve` operation. The name service supports four operations to create bindings: *bind, rebind, bind_context* and *rebind_context*.

```
void bind(in Name n, in Object obj)
    raises(NotFound, CannotProceed, InvalidName, AlreadyBound);
void rebind(in Name n, in Object obj)
    raises(NotFound, CannotProceed, InvalidName);
void bind_context(in Name n, in NamingContext nc)
    raises(NotFound, CannotProceed, InvalidName, AlreadyBound);
void rebind_context(in Name n, in NamingContext nc)
    raises(NotFound, CannotProceed, InvalidName);
```

bind

Creates a binding of a name and an object in the naming context. Naming contexts that are bound using `bind` do not participate in name resolution when compound names are passed to be resolved.

A `bind` operation that is passed a compound name is defined as follows:

ctx->bind(< c1 ; c2 ; ... ; cn >, obj) ≡
(ctx->resolve(< c1 ; c2 ; ... ; cn-1 >))->bind(< cn >, obj)

rebind
Creates a binding of a name and an object in the naming context even if the name is already bound in the context. Naming contexts that are bound using `rebind` do not participate in name resolution when compound names are passed to be resolved.

bind_context
Names an object that is a naming context. Naming contexts that are bound using `bind_context`() participate in name resolution when compound names are passed to be resolved.

A `bind_context` operation that is passed a compound name is defined as follows:

ctx->bind_context(< c1 ; c2 ; ... ; cn >, nc) ≡
(ctx->resolve(< c1 ; c2 ; ... ; cn-1 >))->bind_context(< cn >, nc)

rebind_context
Creates a binding of a name and a naming context in the naming context even if the name is already bound in the context. Naming contexts that are bound using `rebind_context`() participate in name resolution when compound names are passed to be resolved.

Table 3-1 describes the exceptions raised by the binding operations.

Table 3-1 Exceptions Raised by Binding Operations

Exception Raised	Description
NotFound	Indicates the name does not identify a binding.
CannotProceed	Indicates that the implementation has given up for some reason. The client, however, may be able to continue the operation at the returned naming context.
InvalidName	Indicates the name is invalid. (A name of length 0 is invalid; implementations may place other restrictions on names.)
AlreadyBound	Indicates an object is already bound to the specified name. Only one object can be bound to a particular name in a context. The `bind` and the `bind_context` operations raise the `AlreadyBound` exception if the name is bound in the context; the `rebind` and rebind_context operations unbind the name and rebind the name to the object passed as an argument.

3.2.2 Resolving Names

The `resolve` operation is the process of retrieving an object bound to a name in a given context. The given name must exactly match the bound name. The naming service does not return the type of the object. Clients are responsible for "narrowing" the object to the appropriate type. That is, clients typically cast the returned object from Object to a more specialized interface. The IDL definition of the `resolve` operation is:

```
Object resolve (in Name n)
     raises (NotFound, CannotProceed, InvalidName);
```

Names can have multiple components; therefore, name resolution can traverse multiple contexts. A compound resolve is defined as follows:

ctx->resolve(< c1 ; c2 ; ... ; cn >) ≡
ctx->resolve(< c1 ; c2 ; ... ; cn-1 >)->resolve(< cn >)

Table 3-2 describes the exceptions raised by the `resolve` operation.

Table 3-2 Exceptions Raised by Resolve Operation

Exception Raised	Description
NotFound	Indicates the name does not identify a binding.
CannotProceed	Indicates that the implementation has given up for some reason. The client, however, may be able to continue the operation at the returned naming context.
InvalidName	Indicates the name is invalid. (A name of length 0 is invalid; implementations may place other restrictions on names.)

3.2.3 *Unbinding Names*

The `unbind` operation removes a name binding from a context. The definition of the `unbind` operation is:

```
void unbind(in Name n)
     raises (NotFound, CannotProceed, InvalidName);
```

A `unbind` operation that is passed a compound name is defined as follows:

ctx->unbind(< c1 ; c2 ; ... ; cn >) ≡
(ctx->resolve(< c1 ; c2 ; ... ; cn-1 >))->unbind(< cn >)

Table 3-3 describes the exceptions raised by the `unbind` operation.

Table 3-3 Exceptions Raised by Unbind Operation

Exception Raised	Description
NotFound	Indicates the name does not identify a binding.
CannotProceed	Indicates that the implementation has given up for some reason. The client, however, may be able to continue the operation at the returned naming context.
InvalidName	Indicates the name is invalid. (A name of length 0 is invalid; implementations may place other restrictions on names.)

3.2.4 *Creating Naming Contexts*

The name service supports two operations to create new contexts: *new_context* and *bind_new_context*.

```
NamingContext new_context();

NamingContext bind_new_context(in Name n)
raises(NotFound, AlreadyBound, CannotProceed, InvalidName);
```

new_context
: This operation returns a naming context implemented by the same naming server as the context on which the operation was invoked. The new context is not bound to any name.

bind_new_context
: This operation creates a new context and binds it to the name supplied as an argument. The newly created context is implemented by the same naming server as the context in which it was bound (that is, the naming server that implements the context denoted by the name argument excluding the last component).

A `bind_new_context` that is passed a compound name is defined as follows:

ctx->bind_new_context(< c1 ; c2 ; ... ; cn >) ≡
(ctx->resolve(< c1 ; c2 ; ... ; cn-1 >))->bind_new_context(< cn >)

Table 3-4 describes the exceptions raised when new contexts are being created.

Table 3-4 Exceptions Raised When Creating New Contexts

Exception Raised	Description
NotFound	Indicates the name does not identify a binding.
CannotProceed	Indicates that the implementation has given up for some reason. The client, however, may be able to continue the operation at the returned naming context.
InvalidName	Indicates the name is invalid. (A name of length 0 is invalid; implementations may place other restrictions on names.)
AlreadyBound	Indicates an object is already bound to the specified name. Only one object can be bound to a particular name in a context.

3.2.5 *Deleting Contexts*

The `destroy` operation deletes a naming context:.

```
void destroy()
    raises(NotEmpty);
```

If the naming context contains bindings, the `NotEmpty` exception is raised.

3.2.6 *Listing a Naming Context*

The `list` operation allows a client to iterate through a set of bindings in a naming context.

```
enum BindingType {object, ncontext};

struct Binding {
    Name    binding_name;
    BindingType binding_type;
};

typedef sequence <Binding> BindingList;

void list (in unsigned long how_many,
                out BindingList bl, out BindingIterator bi);
};
```

The `list` operation returns at most the requested number of bindings in `BindingList bl`.

- If the naming context contains additional bindings, the `list` operation returns a `BindingIterator` with the additional bindings.

- If the naming context does not contain additional bindings, the binding iterator is a nil object reference.

3.2.7 The BindingIterator Interface

The *BindingIterator* interface allows a client to iterate through the bindings using the next_one or next_n operations:

```
interface BindingIterator {
    boolean next_one(out Binding b);
    boolean next_n(in unsigned long how_many,
                out BindingList bl);
    void destroy();
};
```

next_one
This operation returns the next binding. If there are no more bindings, *false* is returned.

next_n
This operation returns at most the requested number of bindings.

destroy
This operation destroys the iterator.

3.3 The Names Library

To allow the representation of names to evolve without affecting existing clients, it is desirable to hide the representation of names from client code. Ideally, names themselves would be objects; however, names must be lightweight entities that are efficient to create, manipulate, and transmit. As such, names are presented to programs through the *names library.*

The names library implements names as *pseudo-objects*. A client makes calls on a pseudo-object in the same way it makes calls on an ordinary object. Library names are described in pseudo-IDL (to suggest the appropriate language binding). C and C++ clients[2] use the same client language bindings for pseudo-IDL (PIDL) as they use for IDL.

Pseudo-object references cannot be passed across IDL interfaces. As described in Section 3.2, "The CosNaming Module," the naming service supports the *NamingContext* IDL interface. The names library supports an operation to convert a library name into a value that can be passed to the name service through the *NamingContext* interface.

2. As anticipated.

Note – It is not a requirement to use the names library in order to use the name service.

The naming library consists of two pseudo-IDL interfaces: the *LNameComponent* interface and the *LName* interface, as shown in Figure 3-3.

```
interface LNameComponent {     // PIDL
    exception NotSet{};
    string get_id()
        raises(NotSet);
    void set_id(in string i);
    string get_kind()
        raises(NotSet);
    void set_kind(in string k);
    void destroy();
};

interface LName {                              // PIDL
    exception NoComponent{};
    exception OverFlow{};
    exception InvalidName{};
    LName insert_component(in unsigned long i,
                    in LNameComponent n)
            raises(NoComponent, OverFlow);
    LNameComponent get_component(in unsigned long i)
         raises(NoComponent);
    LNameComponent delete_component(in unsigned long i)
         raises(NoComponent);
    unsigned long num_components();
    boolean equal(in LName ln);
    boolean less_than(in LName ln);
    Name to_idl_form()
            raises(InvalidName);
    void from_idl_form(in Name n);
    void destroy();
};

LName create_lname();                          // C/C++
LNameComponent create_lname_component(); // C/C++
```

Figure 3-3 The names library interface in PIDL

3.3.1 Creating a Library Name Component

To create a library name component pseudo-object, use the following C/C++ function:

```
LNameComponent create_lname_component();      // C/C++
```

The returned pseudo-object can then be operated on using the operations in Figure 3-3.

3.3.2 Creating a Library Name

To create a library name pseudo-object, use the following C/C++ function.

```
LName create_lname();                         // C/C++
```

The returned pseudo-object reference can then be operated on using the operations in Figure 3-3.

3.3.3 The LNameComponent Interface

A name component consists of two attributes: the `identifier` attribute and the `kind` attribute. The *LNameComponent* interface defines the operations associated with these attributes.

```
string get_id()
    raises(NotSet);
void set_id(in string k);
string get_kind()
    raises(NotSet);
void set_kind(in string k);
```

get_id
: The `get_id` operation returns the `identifier` attribute's value. If the attribute has not been set, the `NotSet` exception is raised.

set_id
: The `set_id` operation sets the `identifier` attribute to the string argument.

get_kind
: The `get_kind` operation returns the `kind` attribute's value. If the attribute has not been set, the `NotSet` exception is raised.

set_kind

The `set_kind` operation sets the `kind` attribute to the string argument.

3.3.4 The LName Interface

The following operations are described in this section:

- destroying a library name component pseudo-object
- creating a library name
- inserting a name component
- getting the ith name component
- deleting a name component
- number of name components
- testing for equality
- testing for order
- producing an idl form
- translating an idl form
- destroying a library name pseudo-object

Destroying a Library Name Component Pseudo-Object

The `destroy` operation destroys library name component pseudo-objects.

```
void destroy();
```

Inserting a Name Component

A name has one or more components. Each component except the last is used to identify names of subcontexts. (The last component denotes the bound object.) The `insert_component` operation inserts a component after position *i*.

```
LName insert_component(in unsigned long i, in LNameComponent lnc)
    raises(NoComponent, OverFlow);
```

If component *i*-1 is undefined and component *i* is greater than 1, the `insert_component` operation raises the `NoComponent` exception.

If the library cannot allocate resources for the inserted component, the `OverFlow` exception is raised.

Getting the ith Name Component

The get_component operation returns the ith component. The first component is numbered *1*.

```
LNameComponent get_component(in unsigned long i)
    raises(NoComponent);
```

If the component does not exist, the NoComponent exception is raised.

Deleting a Name Component

The delete_component operation removes and returns the ith component.

```
LNameComponent delete_component(in unsigned long i)
    raises(NoComponent);
```

If the component does not exist, the NoComponent exception is raised.

After a delete_component operation has been performed, the compound name has one fewer component and components previously identified as *i+1...n* are now identified as *i...n-1*.

Number of Name Components

The num_components operation returns the number of components in a library name.

```
unsigned long num_components();
```

Testing for Equality

The equal operation tests for equality with library name ln.

```
boolean equal(in LName ln);
```

Testing for Order

The `less_than` operation tests for the order of a library name in relation to library name ln.

```
boolean less_than(in LName ln);
```

This operation returns *true* if the library name is less than the library name ln passed as an argument. The library implementation defines the ordering on names.

Producing an IDL form

Pseudo-objects cannot be passed across IDL interfaces. The library name is a pseudo-object; therefore, it cannot be passed across the IDL interface for the naming service. Several operations in the *NamingContext* interface have arguments of an IDL-defined structure, `Name`. The following PIDL operation on library names produces a structure that can be passed across the IDL request.

```
Name to_idl_form()
    raises(InvalidName);
```

If the name is of length 0, the `InvalidName` exception is returned.

Translating an IDL Form

Pseudo-objects cannot be passed across IDL interfaces. The library name is a pseudo-object; therefore, it cannot be passed across the IDL interface for the naming service. The *NamingContext* interface defines operations that return an IDL struct of type `Name`. The following PIDL operation on library names sets the components and `kind` attribute for a library name from a returned IDL defined structure, `Name`.

```
void from_idl_form(in Name n);
```

Destroying a Library Name Pseudo-Object

The `destroy` operation destroys library name pseudo-objects.

```
void destroy();
```

Event Service Specification 4

4.1 *Service Description*

4.1.1 *Overview*

A standard CORBA request results in the synchronous execution of an operation by an object. If the operation defines parameters or return values, data is communicated between the client and the server. A request is directed to a particular object. For the request to be successful, both the client and the server must be available. If a request fails because the server is unavailable, the client receives an exception and must take some appropriate action.

In some scenarios, a more decoupled communication model between objects is required. For example:

- A system administration tool is interested in knowing if a disk runs out of space. The software managing a disk is unaware of the existence of the system administration tool. The software simply reports that the disk is full. When a disk runs out of space, the system administration tool opens a window to inform the user which disk has run out of space.
- A property list object is associated with an application object. The property list object is physically separate from the application object. The application object is interested in the changes made to its properties by a user. The properties can be changed without involving the application object. That is, in order to have reasonable response time for the user, changing a property does not activate the application object. However, when the application object is activated, it needs to know about the changes to its properties.
- A CASE tool is interested in being notified when a source program has been modified. The source program simply reports when it is modified. It is unaware of the existence of the CASE tool. In response to the notification, the CASE tool invokes a compiler.

- Several documents are linked to a spreadsheet. The documents are interested in knowing when the value of certain cells have changed. When the cell value changes, the documents update their presentations based on the spreadsheet. Furthermore, if a document is unavailable because of a failure, it is still interested in any changes to the cells and wants to be notified of those changes when it recovers.

4.1.2 Event Communication

The event service decouples the communication between objects. The event service defines two roles for objects: the supplier role and the consumer role. *Suppliers* produce event data and *consumers* process event data. Event data are communicated between suppliers and consumers by issuing standard CORBA requests.

There are two approaches to initiating event communication between suppliers and consumers, and two orthogonal approaches to the form that the communication can take.

The two approaches to initiating event communication are called the *push model* and the *pull model*. The push model allows a supplier of events to initiate the transfer of the event data to consumers. The pull model allows a consumer of events to request the event data from a supplier. In the push model, the supplier is taking the initiative; in the pull model, the consumer is taking the initiative.

The communication itself can be either *generic* or *typed*. In the generic case, all communication is by means of generic `push` or `pull` operations that take a single parameter that packages all the event data. In the typed case, communication is via operations defined in IDL. Event data is passed by means of the parameters, which can be defined in any manner desired. Sections 4.2 through 4.5 discuss generic event communication in detail; sections 4.6 through 4.9 discuss typed event communication in detail.

An *event channel* is an intervening object that allows multiple suppliers to communicate with multiple consumers asynchronously. An event channel is both a consumer and a supplier of events. Event channels are standard CORBA objects and communication with an event channel is accomplished using standard CORBA requests.

4.1.3 Example Scenario

This section provides a general scenario that illustrates how the event service can be used.

The event service can be used to provide "change notification." When an object is changed (e.g., its state is modified), an event can be generated that is propagated to all interested parties. For example, when a spreadsheet cell object is modified, all compound documents which contain a reference (link) to that cell can be notified (so the document can redisplay the referenced cell, or recalculate values that depend on the cell). Similarly, when an engineering specification object is modified, all engineers who have registered an interest in the specification can be notified that the specification has changed.

In this scenario, objects that can be "changed" act as suppliers, parties interested in receiving notifications of changes act as consumers, and one or more event channel objects are used as intermediaries between consumers and suppliers. *Either the push or the pull model can be used at either end.*

If the push model is used by suppliers, objects that can be changed support the *PushSupplier* interface so that event communication can be discontinued, use the *EventChannel*, the *SupplierAdmin* and the *ProxyPushConsumer* interfaces to register as suppliers of events, and use the *ProxyPushConsumer* interface to push events to event channels.

When a change occurs to an object, a changeable object invokes a `push` operation on the channel. It provides as an argument to the `push` operation information that describes the event. This information is of data type `any`—it can be as simple or as complex as is necessary. For example, the event information might identify the object reference of the object that has been changed, it might identify the kind of change that has occurred, it might provide a new displayable image of the changed object or it might identify one or more additional objects that describe the change that has been made.

On the consumer side if the pull model is used by consumers, all client objects which are interested in being notified of changes support the *PullConsumer* interface so communication can be discontinued, use the *EventChannel*, *ConsumerAdmin* and *ProxyPullSupplier* interfaces to register as consumers of events, and use the *ProxyPullSupplier* interface to pull events from event channels.

The consumer may use either a blocking or nonblocking mechanism for receiving notification of changes. Using the `try_pull` operation, the consumer can periodically poll the channel for events. Alternatively, the consumer can use the `pull` operation which will block the consumer's execution thread until an event is generated by some supplier.

Event channels act as the intermediaries between the objects being changed and objects interested in knowing about changes. The channels that provide change notification can be general purpose, well-known objects (e.g., "persistent server-based objects" that are run as part of a workgroup-wide framework of objects that provide "desktop services") or specific-to-task objects (e.g., temporary objects that are created when needed). Objects that use event channels may locate the channels by looking for them in a persistently available server (e.g., by looking for them in a naming service) or they may be given references to these objects as part of a specific-to-task object protocol (e.g., when an "open" operation is invoked on an object, the object may return the reference to an event channel which the caller should use until the object is closed).

Event channels determine how changes are propagated between suppliers and consumers, i.e., the qualities of service (Section 4.1.6). For example, an event channel determines the persistence of an event. The channel may keep an event for a specified period of time, passing it along to any consumer who registers with the channel during that period of time (e.g., it may keep event notifications about changes to engineering specifications for a week). Alternatively, the channel may only pass on events to consumers who are currently waiting for notification of changes (e.g., notifications of changes to a spreadsheet cell may only be sent to consumers who are currently displaying that cell).

This scenario exemplifies one way the event service described here forms a basic building block used in providing higher-level services specific to an application or common facilities framework of objects.

Instead of using the generic event channel, a typed event channel could also have been used.

4.1.4 Design Principles

The service design satisfies the following principles:

1. Events work in a distributed environment. The design does not depend on any global, critical, or centralized service.
2. Event services allow multiple consumers of an event and multiple event suppliers.
3. Consumers can either request events or be notified of events, whichever is more appropriate for application design and performance.
4. Consumers and suppliers of events support standard IDL interfaces; no extensions to CORBA are necessary to define these interfaces.
5. A supplier can issue a single standard request to communicate event data to all consumers at once.
6. Suppliers can generate events without knowing the identities of the consumers. Conversely, consumers can receive events without knowing the identities of the suppliers.
7. The event interface allows multiple qualities of service (e.g., for different levels of reliability), and allows for future interface extensions (e.g., for additional functionality).
8. The event service interfaces are capable of being implemented and used in different operating environments (e.g., in environments which support threading and environments which do not support threading).

4.1.5 Resolution of Technical Issues

This specification addresses the issues identified for event services in the OMG *Object Services Architecture*[1] document as follows:

- *Distributed environment*: The interfaces are designed to allow consumers and suppliers of events to be disconnected from time to time, and do not require centralized event identification, processing, routing, or other services that might be a bottleneck or a single point of failure.

  Events themselves are *not* objects because the CORBA distributed object model does not support passing objects by value.

- *Event generation*: The specification describes how events are generated and delivered in a very general fashion, with event channels as intermediate routing points. It does not require (or preclude) polling, nor does it require that an event supplier directly notify every interested party.

- *Events involving multiple objects*: Complex events may be handled by constructing a notification tree of event consumer/suppliers checking for successively more specific event predicates. The specification does not require a general or global event predicate evaluation service as this may not be sufficiently reliable, efficient, or secure in a distributed, heterogeneous (potentially decoupled) environment.

- *Scoping, grouping, and filtering events*: The specification takes advantage of CORBA's distributed scoping and grouping mechanisms for the identifier and type of events. Event filtering is easily achieved through event channels that selectively deliver events from suppliers to consumers. Event channels can be composed; that is, one event channel can consumer events supplied by another.

  Typed event channels can provide filtering based on event type.

- *Registration and generation of events*: Consumers and suppliers register with event channels themselves. Event channels are objects and they are found by any fashion that objects can be found. A global registration service is not required; any object that conforms to the IDL interface specification may consume an event.

- *Event parameters*: The specification supports a parameter of type `any` that can be delivered with an event, used for application-specific data.

- *Forgery and secure events*: Because event suppliers are objects, the specification leverages any ORB work on security for object references and communication.

- *Performance*: The design is a minimalist one, and requires only one ORB call per event received. It supports both push-style and pull-style notification to avoid inefficient event polling. Since event suppliers, consumers, and channels are all ORB objects, the service directly benefits from a Library Object Adapter or any other ORB optimizations.

---

1. *Object Services Architecture*, Document Number 92-8-4, Object Managment Group, Framingham, MA, 1992.

Additional issues that have been taken into account in the design of the event service include:

- Formalized Event Information: For specific application environments and frameworks it may be beneficial to formalize the data associated with an event (defined in this specification as type `any`). This can be accomplished by defining a typed structure for this information. Depending on the needs of the environment, the kinds of information included might be a priority, timestamp, origin string, and confirmation indicator. This information might be solely for the benefit of the event consumer or might also be interpreted by particular event channel implementations.
- Confirmation of Reception: Some applications may require that consumers of an event provide an explicit confirmation of reception back to the supplier. This can be supported effectively using a "reverse" event channel through which consumers send back confirmations as normal events. This obviates the need for any special confirmation mechanism. However, strict atomic delivery between all suppliers and all consumers requires additional interfaces.

4.1.6 *Quality of Service*

Application domains requiring event-style communication have diverse *reliability* requirements, from "at-most-once" semantics (i.e., best effort) to guaranteed "exactly-once" semantics, *availability* requirements, *throughput* requirements, *performance* requirements (i.e., how fast events are disseminated), and *scalability* requirements.

Clearly no single implementation of an event service can optimize such a diverse range of technical requirements. Hence, multiple implementations of event services are to be expected, with different services targeted toward different environments. As such, the event interfaces do not dictate *qualities of service*. Different implementations of the event interfaces can support different qualities of service to meet different application needs.

For example, an implementation that trades at-most-once delivery to a single consumer in favor of performance is useful for some applications; an implementation that favors performance but cannot preclude duplicate delivery is useful for other applications. Both are acceptable implementations of the interfaces described in this chapter.

Clearly, an implementation of an event channel that discards all events is *not a useful* implementation. Useful implementations will at least support "best-effort" delivery of events.

Note that the interfaces defined in this chapter are incomplete for implementations that support strict notions of atomicity. That is, additional interfaces are needed by an implementation to guarantee that either all consumers receive an event or none of the consumers receive an event; and that all events are received in the same order by all consumers.

4.2 Generic Event Communication

There are two basic models for communicating event data between suppliers and consumers: the *push model* and the *pull model.*

4.2.1 Push Model

In the push model, suppliers "push" event data to consumers; that is, suppliers communicate event data by invoking `push` operations on the *PushConsumer* interface.

To set up a push-style communication, consumers and suppliers exchange *PushConsumer* and *PushSupplier* object references. Event communication can be broken by invoking a `disconnect_push_consumer` operation on the *PushConsumer* interface or by invoking a `disconnect_push_supplier` operation on the *PushSupplier* interface. If the *PushSupplier* object reference is nil, the connection cannot be broken via the supplier.

Figure 4-1 illustrates push-style communication between a supplier and a consumer.

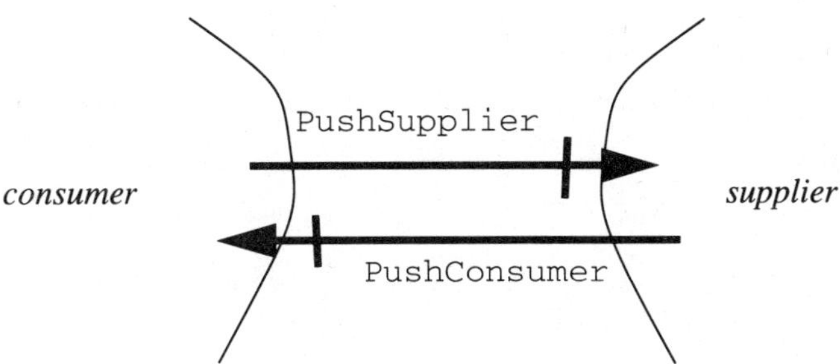

Figure 4-1 Push-style communication between a supplier and a consumer

4.2.2 Pull Model

In the pull model, consumers "pull" event data from suppliers; that is, consumers request event data by invoking `pull` operations on the *PullSupplier* interface.

To set up a pull-style communication, consumers and suppliers must exchange *PullConsumer* and *PullSupplier* object references. Event communication can be broken by invoking a `disconnect_pull_consumer` operation on the *PullConsumer* interface or by invoking a `disconnect_pull_supplier` operation on the *PullSupplier* interface. If the *PullConsumer* object reference is nil, the connection cannot be broken via the consumer.

Figure 4-2 illustrates pull-style communication between a supplier and a consumer.

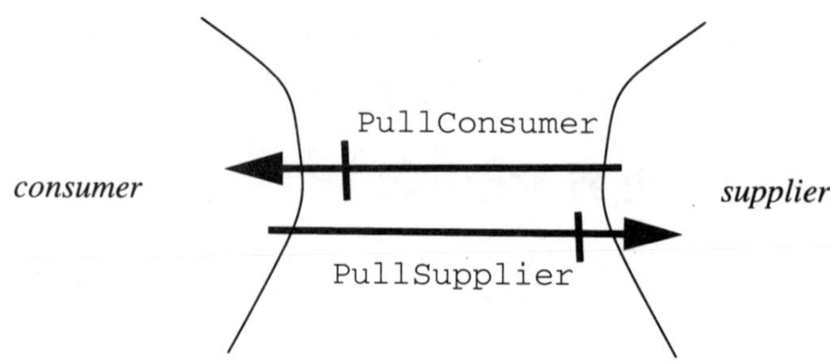

Figure 4-2 Pull-style communication between a supplier and a consumer

4.3 The CosEventComm Module

Names of all IDC modules which form the Common Object Services Specification are prefixed with the initials "Cos."

The communication styles shown in Figures 4-1 and 4-2 are both supported by four simple interfaces: *PushConsumer, PushSupplier,* and *PullSupplier* and *PullConsumer.* These interfaces are defined in an IDL module named `CosEventComm`, as shown in Figure 4-3.

```
module CosEventComm {

    exception Disconnected{};

    interface PushConsumer {
        void push (in any data) raises(Disconnected);
        void disconnect_push_consumer();
    };

    interface PushSupplier {
        void disconnect_push_supplier();
    };

    interface PullSupplier {
        any pull () raises(Disconnected);
        any try_pull (out boolean has_event)
            raises(Disconnected);
        void disconnect_pull_supplier();
    };

    interface PullConsumer {
        void disconnect_pull_consumer();
    };

};
```

Figure 4-3 The IDL module `CosEventComm`

4.3.1 The PushConsumer Interface

A push-style consumer supports the *PushConsumer* interface to receive event data.

```
    interface PushConsumer {
        void push (in any data) raises(Disconnected);
        void disconnect_push_consumer();
    };
```

A supplier communicates event data to the consumer by invoking the `push` operation and passing the event data as a parameter. If the event communication has already been disconnected, the `Disconnected` exception is raised.

The `disconnect_push_consumer` operation terminates the event communication; it releases resources used at the consumer to support the event communication. The *PushConsumer* object reference is disposed.

4.3.2 The PushSupplier Interface

A push-style supplier supports the *PushSupplier* interface.

```
interface PushSupplier {
    void disconnect_push_supplier();
};
```

The `disconnect_push_supplier` operation terminates the event communication; it releases resources used at the supplier to support the event communication. The *PushSupplier* object reference is disposed.

4.3.3 The PullSupplier Interface

A pull-style supplier supports the *PullSupplier* interface to transmit event data.

```
interface PullSupplier {
    any pull () raises(Disconnected);
    any try_pull (out boolean has_event)
        raises(Disconnected);
    void disconnect_pull_supplier();
};
```

A consumer requests event data from the supplier by invoking either the `pull` operation or the `try_pull` operation on the supplier.

- The `pull` operation blocks until the event data is available or an exception is raised.[2] It returns the event data to the consumer. If the event communication has already been disconnected, the `Disconnected` exception is raised.
- The `try_pull` operation does not block: If the event data is available, it returns the event data and sets the `has_event` parameter to *true*; if the event is not available, it sets the `has_event` parameter to *false* and the event data is returned as long with an undefined value. If the event communication has already been disconnected, the `Disconnected` exception is raised.

2. This, of course, may be a standard CORBA exception.

The disconnect_pull_supplier operation terminates the event communication; it releases resources used at the supplier to support the event communication. The *PullSupplier* object reference is disposed.

4.3.4 The PullConsumer Interface

A pull-style consumer supports the *PullConsumer* interface.

```
interface PullConsumer {
    void disconnect_pull_consumer();
};
```

The disconnect_pull_consumer operation terminates the event communication; it releases resources used at the consumer to support the event communication. The *PullConsumer* object reference is disposed.

4.4 Event Channels

The *event channel* is a service that decouples the communication between suppliers and consumers. The event channel is itself both a consumer and a supplier of the event data.

An event channel can provide asynchronous communication of event data between suppliers and consumers. Although consumers and suppliers communicate with the event channel using standard CORBA requests, the event channel does not need to supply the event data to its consumer at the same time it consumes the data from its supplier.

4.4.1 Push-Style Communication with an Event Channel

The supplier pushes event data to the event channel; the event channel, in turn, pushes event data to the consumer. Figure 4-4 illustrates a push-style communication between a supplier and the event channel, and a consumer and the event channel.

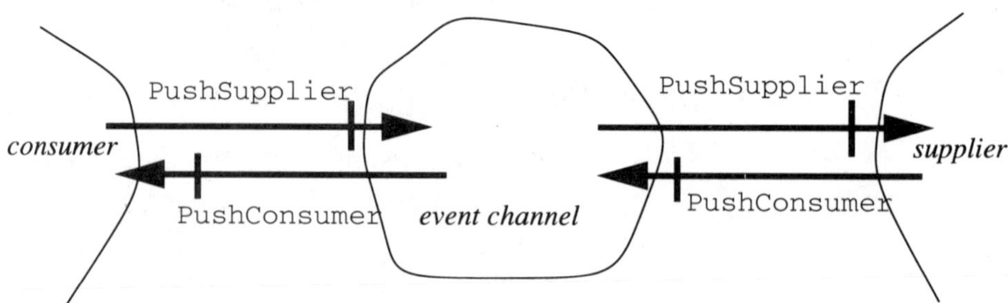

Figure 4-4 Push-style communication between a supplier and an event channel, and a consumer and an event channel

4.4.2 *Pull-Style Communication with an Event Channel*

The consumer pulls event data from the event channel; the event channel, in turn, pulls event data from the supplier. Figure 4-5 illustrates a pull-style communication between a supplier and the event channel, and a consumer and the event channel.

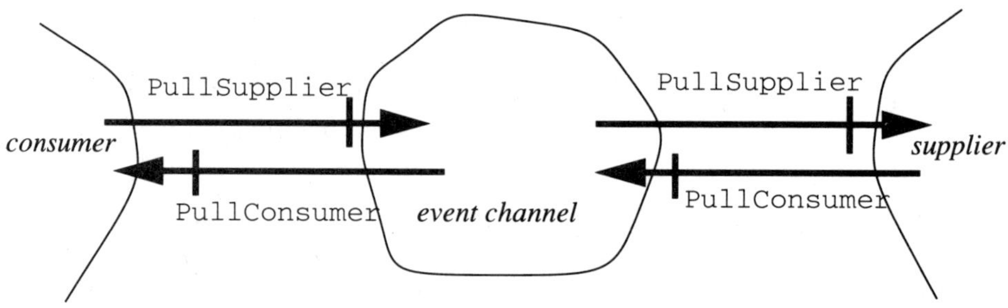

Figure 4-5 Pull-style communication between a supplier and an event channel and a consumer and the event channel

4.4.3 *Mixed-Style Communication with an Event Channel*

An event channel can communicate with a supplier using one style of communication, and communicate with a consumer using a different style of communication.

Figure 4-6 illustrates a push-style communication between a supplier and an event channel, and a pull-style communication between a consumer and the event channel. The consumer pulls the event data that the supplier has pushed to the event channel.

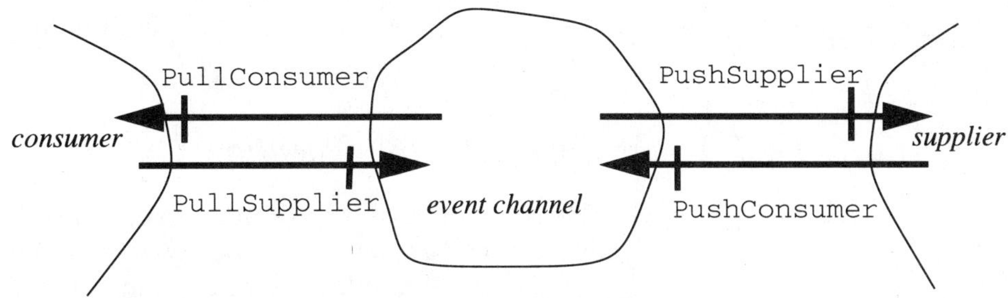

Figure 4-6 Push-style communication between a supplier and an event channel, and pull-style communication between a consumer and an event channel

4.4.4 Multiple Consumers and Multiple Suppliers

Figures 4-4, 4-5, and 4-6 illustrate event channels with a single supplier and a single consumer. An event channel can also provide many-to-many communication. The channel consumes events from one or more suppliers, and supplies events to one or more consumers. Subject to the quality of service of a particular implementation, an event channel provides an event to all consumers.

Figure 4-7 illustrates an event channel with multiple push-style consumers and multiple push-style suppliers.

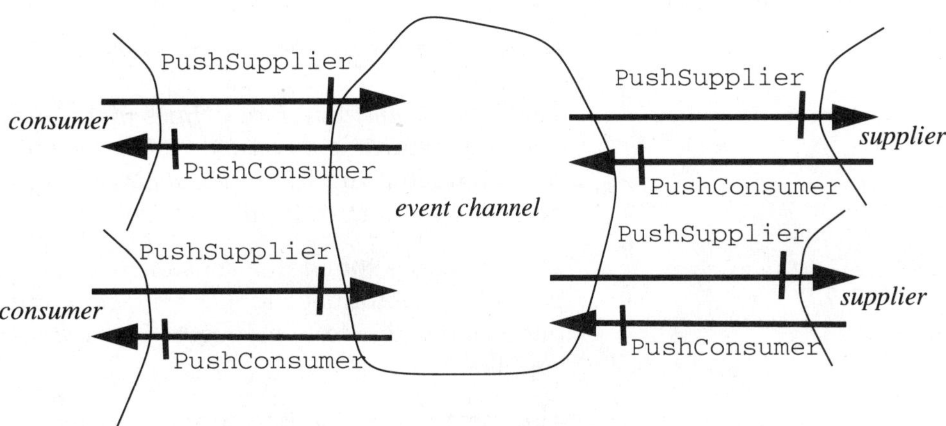

Figure 4-7 An event channel with multiple suppliers and multiple consumers

An event channel can support consumers and suppliers using different communication models.

If an event channel has at least one push-style consumer or at least one pending pull request, the event channel requires an event. If the event channel has pull suppliers, it will issue a request on a pull supplier to satisfy its requirement.

4.4.5 Event Channel Administration

The event channel is built up incrementally. When an event channel is created, no suppliers or consumers are connected to the event channel. Upon creation of the channel, the factory returns an object reference that supports the *EventChannel* interface, as illustrated in Figure 4-8.

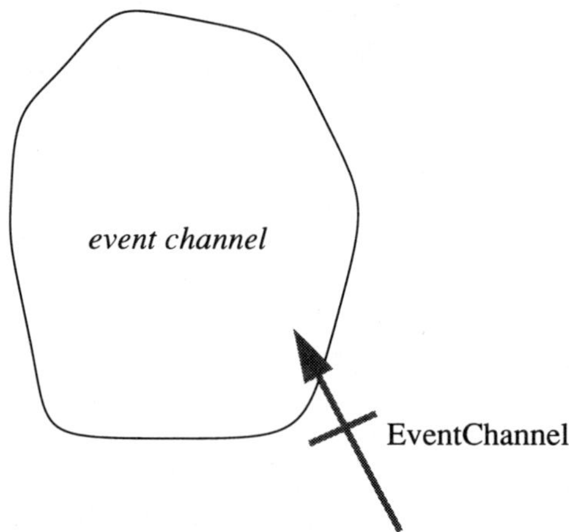

Figure 4-8 A newly created event channel. The channel has no suppliers or consumers.

The *EventChannel* interface defines three administrative operations: an operation returning a *ConsumerAdmin* object for adding consumers, an operation returning a *SupplierAdmin* object for adding suppliers, and an operation for destroying the channel.

The operations for adding consumers return *proxy suppliers*. A proxy supplier is similar to a normal supplier (in fact, it inherits the interface of a supplier), but includes an additional method for connecting a consumer to the proxy supplier.

The operations for adding suppliers return *proxy consumers*. A proxy consumer is similar to a normal consumer (in fact, it inherits the interface of a consumer), but includes an additional method for connecting a supplier to the proxy consumer.

Registration of a producer or consumer is a two-step process. An event-generating application first obtains a proxy consumer from a channel, then "connects" to the proxy consumer by providing it with a supplier. Similarly, an event-receiving application first obtains a proxy supplier from a channel, then "connects" to the proxy supplier by providing it with a consumer.

The reason for the two-step registration process is to support composing event channels by an external agent. Such an agent would compose two channels by obtaining a proxy supplier from one and a proxy consumer from the other, and passing each of them a reference to the other as part of their connect operation.

Proxies are in one of three states: *disconnected, connected* or *destroyed*. Figure 4-9 gives a state diagram for a proxy. The nodes of the diagram are the states and the edges are labelled with the operations that change the state of the proxy. `Push/pull` operations are only valid in the *connected* state.

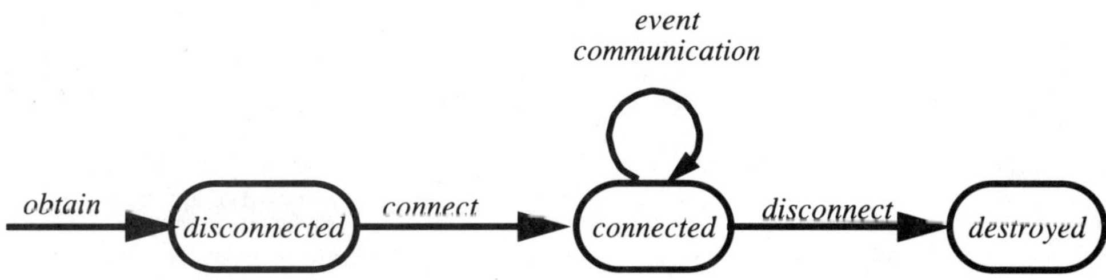

Figure 4-9 State diagram of a proxy

4.5 The CosEventChannelAdmin Module

The `CosEventChannelAdmin` module defines the interfaces for making connections between suppliers and consumers. The `CosEventChannelAdmin` module is defined in Figure 4-10.

```
#include "CosEventComm.idl"

module CosEventChannelAdmin {

    exception AlreadyConnected {};
    exception TypeError {};

    interface ProxyPushConsumer: EventComm::PushConsumer {
        void connect_push_supplier(
                in EventComm::PushSupplier push_supplier)
            raises(AlreadyConnected);
    };

    interface ProxyPullSupplier: EventComm::PullSupplier {
        void connect_pull_consumer(
                in EventComm::PullConsumer pull_consumer)
            raises(AlreadyConnected);
    };

    interface ProxyPullConsumer: EventComm::PullConsumer {
        void connect_pull_supplier(
                in EventComm::PullSupplier pull_supplier)
            raises(AlreadyConnected,TypeError);
    };

    interface ProxyPushSupplier: EventComm::PushSupplier {
        void connect_push_consumer(
                in EventComm::PushConsumer push_consumer)
            raises(AlreadyConnected, TypeError);
    };
```

```
    interface ConsumerAdmin {
        ProxyPushSupplier obtain_push_supplier();
        ProxyPullSupplier obtain_pull_supplier();
    };

    interface SupplierAdmin {
        ProxyPushConsumer obtain_push_consumer();
        ProxyPullConsumer obtain_pull_consumer();
    };

    interface EventChannel {
        ConsumerAdmin for_consumers();
        SupplierAdmin for_suppliers();
        void destroy();
    };

};
```

Figure 4-10 The `CosEventChannelAdmin` module

4.5.1 The EventChannel Interface

The *EventChannel* interface defines three administrative operations: adding consumers, adding suppliers, and destroying the channel.

```
interface EventChannel {
    ConsumerAdmin for_consumers();
    SupplierAdmin for_suppliers();
    void destroy();
};
```

Any object that possesses an object reference that supports the *EventChannel* interface can perform these operations:

- The *ConsumerAdmin* interface allows consumers to be connected to the event channel. The `for_consumers` operation returns an object reference that supports the *ConsumerAdmin* interface.
- The *SupplierAdmin* interface allows suppliers to be connected to the event channel. The `for_suppliers` operation returns an object reference that supports the *SupplierAdmin* interface.
- The `destroy` operation destroys the event channel.

Consumer administration and supplier administration are defined as separate objects so that the creator of the channel can control the addition of suppliers and consumers. For example, a creator might wish to be the sole supplier of event data but allow many consumers to be connected to the channel. In such a case, the creator would simply export the *ConsumerAdmin* object.

4.5.2 The ConsumerAdmin Interface

The *ConsumerAdmin* interface defines the first step for connecting consumers to the event channel; clients use it to obtain proxy suppliers.

```
interface ConsumerAdmin {
    ProxyPushSupplier obtain_push_supplier();
    ProxyPullSupplier obtain_pull_supplier();
};
```

The `obtain_push_supplier` operation returns a *ProxyPushSupplier* object. The *ProxyPushSupplier* object is then used to connect a push-style consumer.

The `obtain_pull_supplier` operation returns a *ProxyPullSupplier* object. The *ProxyPullSupplier* object is then used to connect a pull-style consumer.

4.5.3 The SupplierAdmin Interface

The *SupplierAdmin* interface defines the first step for connecting suppliers to the event channel; clients use it to obtain proxy consumers.

```
interface SupplierAdmin {
    ProxyPushConsumer obtain_push_consumer();
    ProxyPullConsumer obtain_pull_consumer();
};
```

The `obtain_push_consumer` operation returns a *ProxyPushConsumer* object. The *ProxyPushConsumer* object is then used to connect a push-style supplier.

The `obtain_pull_consumer` operation returns a *ProxyPullConsumer* object. The *ProxyPullConsumer* object is then used to connect a pull-style supplier.

4.5.4 The ProxyPushConsumer Interface

The *ProxyPushConsumer* interface defines the second step for connecting push suppliers to the event channel.

```
interface ProxyPushConsumer: EventComm::PushConsumer {
    void connect_push_supplier(
            in EventComm::PushSupplier push_supplier)
        raises(AlreadyConnected);
};
```

A nil object reference may be passed to the `connect_push_supplier` operation; if so, a channel cannot invoke the `disconnect_push_supplier` operation on the supplier; the supplier may be disconnected from the channel without being informed.

If the *ProxyPushConsumer* is already connected to a *PushSupplier*, then the `AlreadyConnected` exception is raised.

4.5.5 The ProxyPullSupplier Interface

The *ProxyPullSupplier* interface defines the second step for connecting pull consumers to the event channel.

```
interface ProxyPullSupplier: EventComm::PullSupplier {
    void connect_pull_consumer(
            in EventComm::PullConsumer pull_consumer)
        raises(AlreadyConnected);
};
```

A nil object reference may be passed to the `connect_pull_consumer` operation; if so, a channel cannot invoke a `disconnect_pull_consumer` operation on the consumer; the consumer may be disconnected from the channel without being informed.

If the *ProxyPullSupplier* is already connected to a *PullConsumer*, then the `AlreadyConnected` exception is raised.

4.5.6 The ProxyPullConsumer Interface

The *ProxyPullConsumer* interface defines the second step for connecting pull suppliers to the event channel.

```
interface ProxyPullConsumer: EventComm::PullConsumer {
    void connect_pull_supplier(
            in EventComm::PullSupplier pull_supplier)
        raises(AlreadyConnected, TypeError);
};
```

Implementations should raise the CORBA standard BAD_PARAM exception if a nil object reference is passed to the `connect_pull_supplier` operation.

If the *ProxyPullConsumer* is already connected to a *PullSupplier*, then the `AlreadyConnected` exception is raised.

An implementation of a *ProxyPullConsumer* may put additional requirements on the interface supported by the pull supplier. If the pull supplier does not meet those requirements the *ProxyPullConsumer* raises the `TypeError` exception. (See section 4.7.2 for an example.)

4.5.7 The ProxyPushSupplier Interface

The *ProxyPushSupplier* interface defines the second step for connecting push consumers to the event channel.

```
interface ProxyPushSupplier: EventComm::PushSupplier {
    void connect_push_consumer(
            in EventComm::PushConsumer push_consumer)
        raises(AlreadyConnected, TypeError);
};
```

Implementations should raise the CORBA standard BAD_PARAM exception if a nil object reference is passed to the `connect_push_consumer` operation.

If the *ProxyPushSupplier* is already connected to a *PushConsumer,* then the `AlreadyConnected` exception is raised.

An implementation of a *ProxyPushSupplier* may put additional requirements on the interface supported by the push consumer. If the push consumer does not meet those requirements the *ProxyPushSupplier* raises the `TypeError` exception. (See section 4.7.1 for an example.)

4.6 Typed Event Communication

Section 4.2 discusses generic event communication using `push` and `pull` operations. The next few sections describe how event communication can be described in IDL and how typed event channels can support such typed event communication.

4.6.1 Typed Push Model

In the typed push model, suppliers call operations on consumers using some mutually agreed interface *I*. The interface *I* is defined in IDL, and may contain any operations subject to the following restrictions:

- All parameters must be `in` parameters only.
- No return values are permitted.

These are the same restrictions as CORBA imposes on `oneway` operations, and for similar reasons: Event communication is unidirectional, and does not directly support responses. The operations can be declared `oneway`, but need not be.

To set up typed push-style communication, consumers and suppliers exchange *TypedPushConsumer* and *PushSupplier* object references. (Note that the supplier interface is the same as the untyped case.) The supplier then invokes the `get_typed_consumer` operation of the *TypedPushConsumer* interface, which returns an object reference supporting the typed interface, *I*, referred to as an *I-reference*. The particular interface, *I*, that the reference supports is dependent on the particular *TypedPushConsumer*, and must be mutually agreed by supplier and consumer. Once the supplier has obtained the *I*-reference, it can call operations in interface *I* on the consumer.

As in the case of the generic push-style, event communication can be broken by invoking a `disconnect_push_consumer` operation on the *TypedPushConsumer* interface or by invoking a `disconnect_push_supplier` operation on the *PushSupplier* interface. If the *PushSupplier* object reference is nil, the connection cannot be broken via the supplier.

Figure 4-11 illustrates typed push-style communication between supplier and consumer.

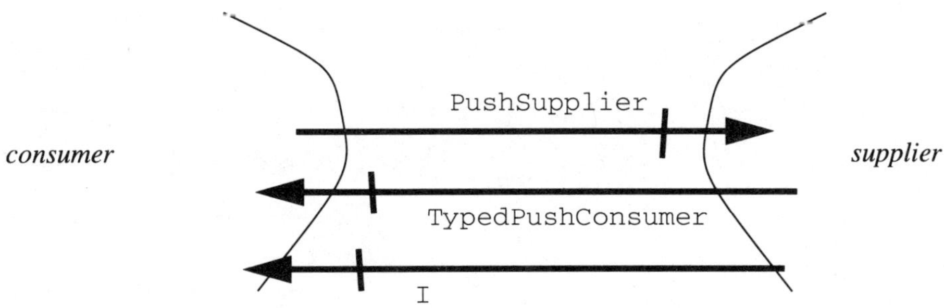

Figure 4-11 Typed push-style communication between a supplier and a consumer

4.6.2 Typed Pull Model

In the typed pull model, consumers call operations on suppliers, requesting event information, using some mutually agreed interface *Pull<I>*.[3] For every interface *I* having the properties described in section 4.6.1, an interface *Pull<I>* is defined as follows:

- For every operation `o` in *I, Pull<I>* contains two operations:
  - `pull_o`, with all `in` parameters changed to `out` parameters. When called, this operation will return with the event data in the *out* parameters. If no *o*-event is currently available, it will block.

3. *Pull<I>* is used as notation for a computed interface from interface I. Thus, if *I* is an interface *DocumentEvents, Pull<I>* is an interface *PullDocumentEvents.*

- `boolean try_o`, with all `in` parameters changed to out parameters. When called, this operation will check whether an *o*-event is currently available. If so, it will return `true`, with the event data in the *out* parameters. If not, it will return `false`, with the `out` parameters undefined.

The interface *Pull<I>* is designed to allow pulling of exactly the same events that can be pushed using interface *I*.

To set up typed pull-style communication, consumers and suppliers exchange *PullConsumer* and *TypedPullSupplier* object references. (Note that the consumer interface is the same as the untyped case.) The consumer then invokes the `get_typed_supplier` operation of the *TypedPullSupplier*, which returns an object reference supporting the typed interface, *Pull<I>*, referred to as a *Pull<I>-reference*. The particular interface, *Pull<I>*, that the reference supports is dependent on the particular *TypedPullSupplier*, and must be mutually agreed by supplier and consumer. Once the consumer has obtained the *Pull<I>-reference*, it can call operations in interface *Pull<I>* on the supplier.

Figure 4-12 illustrates typed pull-style communication between supplier and consumer.

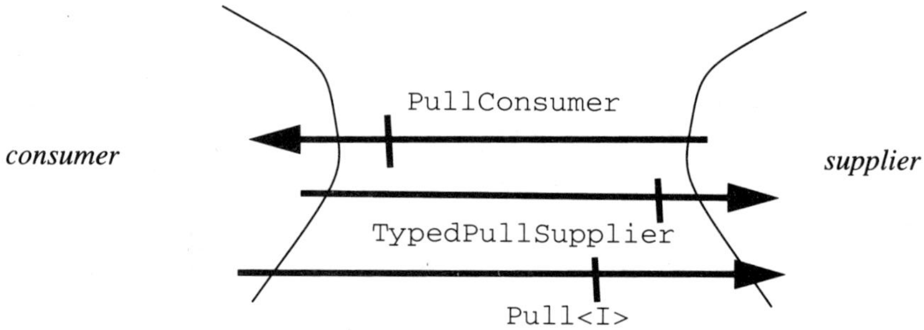

Figure 4-12 Typed pull-style communication between a supplier and a consumer

4.7 The CosTypedEventComm Module

Names of all IDC modules which form the Common Object Service Specification are prefixed with the initials "Cos."

The typed communication styles shown in Figures 4-11 and 4-12 are both supported by two new interfaces, *TypedPushConsumer* and *TypedPullSupplier* and two existing interfaces, *PushSupplier* and *PullConsumer*. The first two interfaces are defined in an IDL module named *CosTypedEventComm,* as shown in Figure 4-13. The last two are the same as for untyped event communication, and were defined in the *CosEventComm* module in Figure 4-3.

```
#include "CosEventComm.idl"

module CosTypedEventComm {

    interface TypedPushConsumer : EventComm::PushConsumer {
        Object get_typed_consumer();
    };

    interface TypedPullSupplier : EventComm::PullSupplier {
        Object get_typed_supplier();
    };

};
```

Figure 4-13 The IDL module `CosTypedEventComm`

4.7.1 The TypedPushConsumer Interface

A typed push-style consumer supports the *TypedPushConsumer* interface both to receive event data in the generic manner, and to supply a specific typed interface through which to receive it in typed form.

```
    interface TypedPushConsumer : EventComm::PushConsumer {
        Object get_typed_consumer();
    };
```

The *TypedPushConsumer* can behave just like an untyped *PushConsumer,* described in section 4.3.1. In addition, if the supplier wishes to communicate event data to the consumer in typed rather than generic form, it first invokes the `get_typed_consumer` operation. This returns an *I-reference* supporting an interface *I*. The particular interface, *I*, that the reference supports is dependent on the particular *TypedPushConsumer.* The return type of the operation is *Object,* because different *TypedPushConsumers* will return references of different types, so the actual type cannot be specified in a general definition. Once the supplier has obtained the *I-reference,* it can narrow it to *I*, and then call operations in interface *I* on the consumer. Mutual agreement about *I* is needed between the supplier and consumer. If they do not agree, the narrow operation will fail.

As noted above, a *TypedPushConsumer* must support the `push` operation, inherited from *EventComm::PushConsumer.* Implementing `push` fully is an unnecessary burden if the consumer is intended for typed use only. It is therefore permissible to implement a *TypedPushConsumer* with a null implementation of push that merely raises the standard CORBA exception NO_IMPLEMENT. Clearly, suppliers must know this and confine themselves to typed communication with such consumers.

4.7.2 The TypedPullSupplier Interface

A typed pull-style supplier supports the *TypedPullSupplier* interface both to allow consumers to pull event data in the generic manner, and to supply a specific typed interface through which they can pull it in typed form.

```
interface TypedPullSupplier : EventComm::PullSupplier {
    Object get_typed_supplier();
};
```

The *TypedPullSupplier* can behave just like an untyped *PullSupplier*, described in section 4.3.3. In addition, if the consumer wishes to pull event data from the supplier in typed rather than generic form, it first invokes the get_typed_supplier operation. This returns a *Pull<I>-reference* supporting an interface *Pull<I>*. The particular interface, *Pull<I>*, that the reference supports is dependent on the particular *TypedPullSupplier.* The return type of the operation is *Object*, because different *TypedPullSuppliers* will return references of different types, so the actual type cannot be specified in a general definition. Once the consumer has obtained the *Pull<I>-reference*, it can narrow it to *Pull<I>*, and then call operations in interface *Pull<I>* on the supplier. Mutual agreement about *Pull<I>* is needed between the supplier and consumer. If they do not agree, the narrow operation will fail.

As noted above, a *TypedPullSupplier* must support the pull and try_pull operations, inherited from *EventComm::PullSupplier.* Implementing these operations fully is an unnecessary burden if the supplier is intended for typed use only. It is therefore permissible to implement a *TypedPullSupplier* with null implementations of pull and try_pull that merely raise the standard CORBA exception NO_IMPLEMENT. Clearly, consumers must know this and confine themselves to typed communication with such suppliers.

4.8 Typed Event Channels

Typed event channels are analogous to generic event channels, but they support both typed and generic event communication. These forms can be mixed at will. A single channel can handle events supplied and consumed in any combination of the forms defined earlier (push/pull, generic/typed). An event supplied in typed form can be consumed in generic form, or vice versa.[4]

4. Doing this does require an understanding on the part of the generic suppliers and consumers of how the channel packages parameters of typed calls when converting them to generic form. Details of this packaging are dependent on the implementation of the channel.

4.9 The CosTypedEventChannelAdmin Module

The `CosTypedEventChannelAdmin` module defines the interfaces for making connections between suppliers and consumers that use either generic or typed communication. It is defined in Figure 4-14. Most of its interfaces are specializations of the corresponding interfaces in the `CosEventChannel` module defined in Figure 4-10.

```
#include "CosEventChannel.idl"
#include "CosTypedEventComm.idl"

module CosTypedEventChannelAdmin {

    exception InterfaceNotSupported {};
    exception NoSuchImplementation {};
    typedef string Key;

    interface TypedProxyPushConsumer :
            EventChannelAdmin::ProxyPushConsumer,
            TypedEventComm::TypedPushConsumer  { };

    interface TypedProxyPullSupplier :
            EventChannelAdmin::ProxyPullSupplier,
            TypedEventComm::TypedPullSupplier { };

    interface TypedSupplierAdmin :
            EventChannelAdmin::SupplierAdmin {
        TypedProxyPushConsumer obtain_typed_push_consumer(
                in Key supported_interface)
            raises(InterfaceNotSupported);
        ProxyPullConsumer obtain_typed_pull_consumer (
                in Key uses_interface)
             raises(NoSuchImplementation);
    };

    interface TypedConsumerAdmin :
            EventChannelAdmin::ConsumerAdmin {
        TypedProxyPullSupplier obtain_typed_pull_supplier(
                in Key supported_interface)
            raises (InterfaceNotSupported);
        ProxyPushSupplier obtain_typed_push_supplier(
                in Key uses_interface)
            raises(NoSuchImplementation);
    };

    interface TypedEventChannel {
        TypedConsumerAdmin for_consumers();
        TypedSupplierAdmin for_suppliers();
        void destroy ();
    };
};
```

Figure 4-14 The `CosTypedEventChannelAdmin` **module**

4.9.1 The TypedEventChannel Interface

```
interface TypedEventChannel {
    TypedConsumerAdmin for_consumers();
    TypedSupplierAdmin for_suppliers();
    void destroy ();
};
```

This interface is analogous to `EventChannelAdmin::EventChannel`. However, it returns typed versions of the consumer and supplier administration interfaces, which are capable of providing proxies for either generic or typed communication.

4.9.2 The TypedConsumerAdmin Interface

The *TypedConsumerAdmin* interface defines the first step for connecting consumers to typed event channel; clients use it to obtain proxy suppliers.

```
interface TypedConsumerAdmin :
        EventChannelAdmin::ConsumerAdmin {
    TypedProxyPullSupplier obtain_typed_pull_supplier(
            in Key supported_interface)
        raises (InterfaceNotSupported);
    ProxyPushSupplier obtain_typed_push_supplier(
            in Key uses_interface)
        raises(NoSuchImplementation);
};
```

The `obtain_typed_pull_supplier` operation takes a Key parameter that identifies an interface, *Pull<I>*. The scope of the key is the typed event channel. It returns a *TypedProxyPullSupplier* for interface *Pull<I>*. The *TypedProxyPullSupplier* will allow an attached pull consumer to pull events either in generic form or using operations in interface *Pull<I>*. It is up to the implementation of `obtain_typed_pull_supplier` to create or find an appropriate *TypedProxyPullSupplier.* If it cannot, it raises the exception `InterfaceNotSupported`.

The `obtain_typed_push_supplier` operation takes a `Key` parameter that identifies an interface, *I.* The scope of the key is the typed event channel. It returns a *ProxyPushSupplier* that calls operations in interface *I*, rather than `push` operations. It is up to the implementation of `obtain_typed_push_supplier` to create or find an appropriate *ProxyPushSupplier.*[5] If it cannot, it raises the exception `NoSuchImplementation`.

5. See Appendix 4A for implementation considerations.

Such a *ProxyPushSupplier* is guaranteed only to invoke operations defined in interface *I*. Any event on the channel that does not correspond to an operation defined in interface *I* is not passed on to the consumer. Such a *ProxyPushSupplier* is therefore an event filter based on type.

4.9.3 The TypedSupplierAdmin Interface

The *TypedSupplierAdmin* interface defines the first step for connecting suppliers to the typed event channel; clients use it to obtain proxy consumers.

```
interface TypedSupplierAdmin :
        EventChannelAdmin::SupplierAdmin {
    TypedProxyPushConsumer obtain_typed_push_consumer(
            in Key supported_interface)
        raises(InterfaceNotSupported);
    ProxyPullConsumer obtain_typed_pull_consumer (
            in Key uses_interface)
         raises(NoSuchImplementation);
};
```

The `obtain_typed_push_consumer` operation takes a `Key` parameter that identifies an interface, *I*. The scope of the key is the typed event channel. It returns a *TypedProxyPushConsumer* for *I*. An attached supplier can provide events by using operations in interface *I*. It is up to the implementation of `obtain_typed_push_consumer` to create or find an appropriate *TypedProxyPushConsumer*. If it cannot, it raises the exception `InterfaceNotSupported`.

The `obtain_typed_pull_consumer` operation takes a `Key` parameter that identifies an interface, *Pull<I>*. The scope of the key is the typed event channel. It returns a *ProxyPullConsumer* that calls operations in interface *Pull<I>*, rather than `pull` operations. It is up to the implementation of `obtain_typed_pull_consumer` to create or find an appropriate *ProxyPullConsumer*. If it cannot, it raises the exception `NoSuchImplementation`.

Such a *ProxyPullConsumer* is guaranteed only to invoke operations defined in interface *Pull<I>*. Any event request that does not correspond to an operation defined in interface *Pull<I>* is not pulled from the supplier. Such a *ProxyPullConsumer* is therefore an event filter based on type.

4.9.4 The TypedProxyPushConsumer Interface

The *TypedProxyPushConsumer* interface defines the second step for connecting push suppliers to the typed event channel.

```
interface TypedProxyPushConsumer :
        EventChannelAdmin::ProxyPushConsumer,
        TypedEventComm::TypedPushConsumer  { };
```

By inheriting from both `EventChannelAdmin::ProxyPushConsumer` and `TypedEventComm::TypedPushConsumer`, this interface supports:

- connection and disconnection of push suppliers, exactly as in the generic event channel,
- generic `push` operation and
- obtaining the typed view, so that the supplier can use typed push communication. The reference returned by `get_typed_consumer` has the interface identified by the `Key` used when this *TypedProxyPushConsumer* was obtained. (See section 4.9.3.)

4.9.5 The TypedProxyPullSupplier Interface

The *TypedProxyPullSupplier* interface defines the second step for connecting pull consumers to the typed event channel.

```
interface TypedProxyPullSupplier :
        EventChannelAdmin::ProxyPullSupplier,
        TypedEventComm::TypedPullSupplier { };
```

By inheriting from both `EventChannelAdmin::ProxyPullSupplier` and `TypedEventComm::TypedPullSupplier`, this interface supports:

- connection and disconnection of pull consumers, exactly as in the generic event channel,
- generic `pull` and `try_pull` operations and
- obtaining the typed view, so that the consumer can use typed pull communication. The reference returned by `get_typed_supplier` supports the interface identified by the `Key` used when this *TypedProxyPullSupplier* was obtained. (See section 4.9.2.)

4.10 Composing Event Channels and Filtering

The event channel administration operations defined in section 4.5 support the composition of event channels. That is, one event channel can consume events supplied by another. This architecture allows the implementation of an event channel that filters the events supplied by another.

Since the *ProxyPushSupplier* for interface *I* of a typed event channel only pushes events that correspond to *I*, it acts as a filter based on type. Similarly, because the *ProxyPullConsumer* for interface *Pull<I>* of a typed event channel only pulls events that correspond to *Pull<I>*, it also acts as a filter based on type.

4.11 Policies for Finding Event Channels

The event service does not establish a policy for finding event channels. Finding a service is orthogonal to using the service. Higher levels of software (such as the desktop) can make policies for using the event channel. That is, higher layers will dictate when an event channel is created and how references to the event channel are obtained. By representing the event channel as an object, it has all of the properties that apply to objects, including support by finding mechanisms.

For example, when a user performs a `drag-and-drop` or `cut-and-paste` operation, an event channel could be created and identified to suppliers and consumers. Alternatively, the event channel could be named in a naming context, or it could be exported through an operation on an object.

Appendix 4A Implementing Typed Event Channels

Note – Implementation details do not form part of an OMG specification, and should not be standardized. On the other hand, it is not obvious that typed channels can be implemented without extensions to CORBA. This section indicates *one* strategy for implementing typed event channels. It is included to show that typed event channels can be implemented; it is not intended in any way to constrain implementations. Optimized implementations are certainly possible.

Figure 4A-1 demonstrates a possible implementation of a typed event channel. This Appendix concentrates on push-style communication. The implementation of pull-style communication is analogous.

The implementation interposes an *encoder* between typed-style suppliers and the channel and a *decoder* between the channel and typed-style consumers.

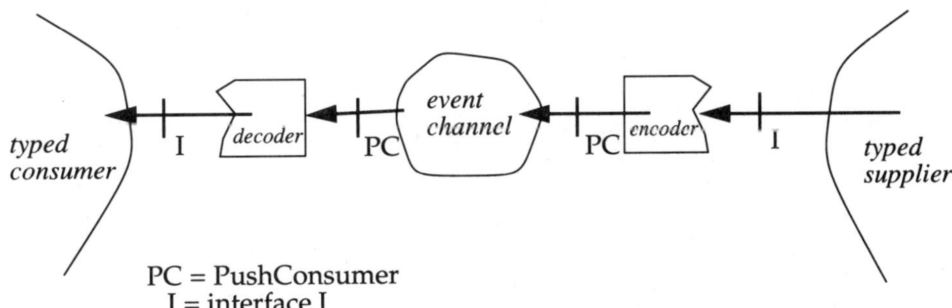

Figure 4A-1 A possible implementation of a typed event channel

At the supplier end, an *encoder* converts operation calls to `push` calls.

At the consumer end, a *decoder* converts `push` calls back to operation calls.

The effect of such a communication is that the original operation is eventually called on the consumer, but the communication is routed via the channel. Of course, there can be multiple suppliers and multiple consumers on the same channel. Whenever one of the suppliers calls an operation, it is delivered by the channel to all consumers.

The encoder must package the operation identification and the parameters in a manner that the decoder can unpack them correctly.

Given the IDL definition of an interface, *I*, an *encoder generator* could generate an implementation that supports the interface *I* and converts all calls on this interface to `push` calls on an event channel. We term such a encoder an I-encoder.

Similarly, it is possible to generate an I-decoder from the IDL definition of I.

The typed event channel is responsible for finding, creating or implementing the appropriate encoders. An appropriate encoder is found or created in response to the `obtain_typed_push_consumer` request on the typed event channel. The encoder is returned in response to the `get_typed_consumer` request.

Similarly, the typed event channel is responsible for finding, creating or implementing the appropriate decoders. An appropriate decoder is found or created in response to the `connect_push_consumer` request on the typed event channel.

Appendix 4B An Event Channel Use Example

This section illustrates an *example* use of the event channel, including the following:

- creating an event channel
- consumers and/or suppliers finding the channel
- suppliers using the event channel

In this example, the document object creates event channels and defines operations in its interface to allow consumers to be added.

- The *Document* interface defines two operations to return event channels:

```
interface Document {
    ConsumerAdmin title_changed();
    ConsumerAdmin new_section();
        :
};
```

The `title_changed` operation causes the document to generate an event when its title is changed; the `new_section` operation causes the document to generate an event when a new section is added. Both operations return *ConsumerAdmin* object references. This allows consumers to be added to the event channel.

- The `title_changed` implementation contains instance variables for using and administering the event channels.

```
/* Factory for creating event channels. */
EventChannelFactoryRef    ecf;

/* For title changed event channel */
EventChannelRef                event_channel;
ConsumerAdminRef              consum_admin;
SupplierAdminRef          supplier_admin;
ProxyPushConsumerRef       proxy_push_consumer;
PushSupplierRef            doc_side_connection;
```

- At some point, the document implementation creates the event channel, gets supplier and consumer administrative references, and adds itself as a supplier.[6]

```
event_channel = ecf->create_eventchannel(env);
supplier_admin = event_channel->for_suppliers(env);
consumer_admin = event_channel->for_consumers(env);
proxy_push_consumer = supplier_admin->obtain_push_consumer(env);
proxy_push_consumer->connect_push_supplier(env,
                                          doc_side_connection)
```

- The `title_changed` operation returns the *ConsumerAdmin* object reference.

```
return consumer_admin;
```

  Clients of this operation can add consumers.

- When the title changes, the document implementation pushes the event to the channel.

```
proxy_push_consumer->push(env,data);
```

The document implementation similarly initializes, exports, and uses the event channel for reporting new sections.

6. For readability, exception handling is omitted from these code fragments.

Life Cycle Services Specification 5

5.1 Service Description

5.1.1 Overview

Life cycle services define services and conventions for creating, deleting, copying and moving objects. Because CORBA-based environments support *distributed* objects, life cycle services define services and conventions that allow clients to perform life cycle operations on objects in different locations.

This chapter begins by describing the life cycle problem for distributed object systems.

The Problem of Creation

Figure 5-1 graphically illustrates the problem of a client in one location creating an object in another.

Figure 5-1 Life cycle service defines how a client can create an object "over there."

To create an object in a different location, the following questions must be answered:

- Can the client control the location for the new object?

- On the other hand, can the location be determined according to some administered policy?
- What entity does the client communicate with in order that a new object is created?
- How does the client find that entity?
- How much control does the client have over deciding the implementation of the created object?
- Can the client influence the initial values of the newly created object?
- Can the client create an object in an implementation-specific fashion?

The Problem of Moving or Copying an Object

Figure 5-2 graphically illustrates the problem of moving or copying an object in a distributed object system.

Figure 5-2 Life cycle services define how a client can move or copy an object "over there."

To support moving or copying an object, we must answer the following questions must be answered:

- Can the client control the location for the copied or migrated object?
- On the other hand, can the location be determined according to some administered policy?
- What entity does the client communicate with to copy or migrate the object?
- How does the client find that entity?
- What happens to the implementation code of a copied or migrated object?

The Problem of Operating on a Graph of Distributed Objects

Distributed objects do not *float* in space; they are connected to one another. The connections are called *relationships. Relationships* allow semantics to be added to references between objects. For example, *relationships* allow one object to *contain* another. Life Cycle services must work in the presence of graphs of related objects.

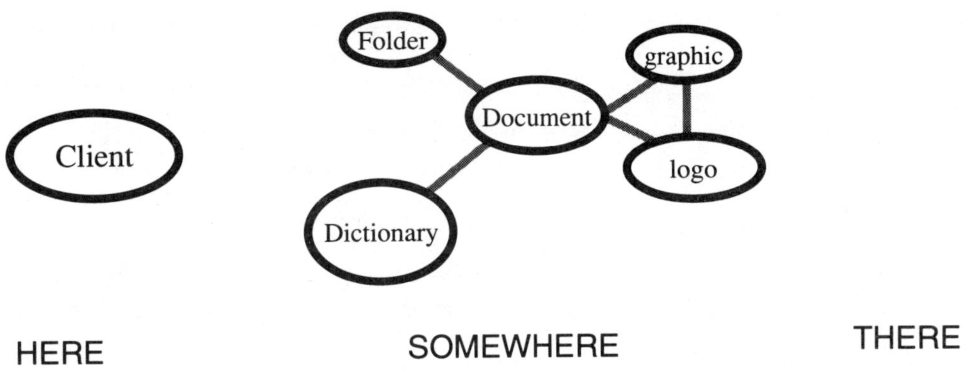

Figure 5-3 The object life cycle problem for graphs of objects is to determine the boundaries of a graph of objects and operate on that graph. In the above example, a document contains a graphic and a logo, refers to a dictionary and is contained in a folder.

Figure 5-3 graphically illustrates the object life cycle problem for graphs of objects. In the example, the folder *contains* a document, the document *contains* a graphic and a logo and *references* a dictionary. The graphic *references* the logo that is *contained* in the document. For graphs of objects, life cycle services must answer the following questions:

- What are the boundaries of the graph? For example, if a client copies the document, which objects are affected?
- If multiple objects are affected, how is the life cycle operation actually applied to those objects?
- Are cycles in the graph preserved? For example, if copying the document results in copying the graphic and the logo, is the cycle preserved in the copy?

5.1.2 *Organization of the Specification*

The remainder of the specification defines services and conventions to answer these life cycle issues.

Section 5.1.3 specifies a *client's model* of object life cycle. It describes the model a client has of factories and life cycle operations. A wide variety of implementations of this model are possible.

Section 5.1.4 discusses *factory finders* in detail.

Section 5.2 defines the *CosLifeCycle* module. This module defines the service interfaces and the interface supported by objects that participate in the service.

Section 5.3 discusses *factory implementation strategies*.

Section 5.4 discusses how objects can use factories and factory finders to support the *copy* and *move* operations.

Section 5.5 summarizes the object life cycle framework.

Appendix 5A through Appendix 5D are not part of the life cycle specification. They are included as background material.

5.1.3 *Client's Model of Object Life Cycle*

A client is any piece of code that initiates a life cycle operation for some object. A client has a *simple* view of the life cycle operations.

Client's Model of Creation

The client's model of creation is defined in terms of *factory* objects. A factory is an object that creates another object. Factories are *not* special objects. As with any object, factories have well-defined IDL interfaces and implementations in some programming language.

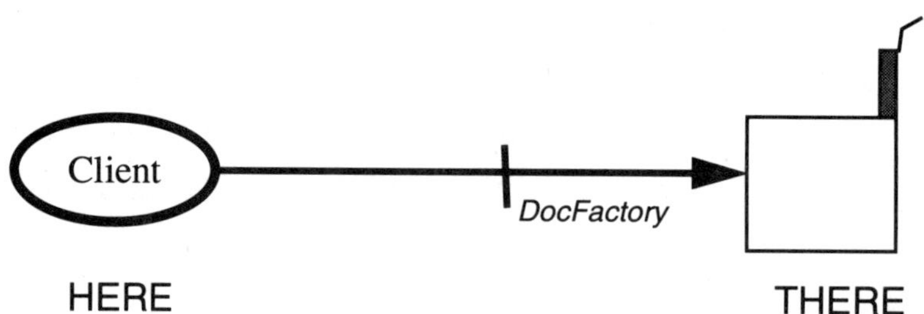

Figure 5-4 To create an object "over there" a client must posses an object reference to a factory over there. The client simply issues a request on the factory.

There is no *standard* interface for a factory. Factories provide the client with specialized operations to create and initialize new instances in a natural way for the implementation. Figure 5-5 illustrates a factory for a document.

```
interface DocFactory {
    Document create();
    Document create_with_title(in string title);
    Document create_for(in natural_language nl);
};
```

Figure 5-5 An example of a document factory interface. This interface is defined for clients as a part of application development.

Factories are object *implementation* dependent. A different implementation of the document could define a different factory interface.

While there is no standard interface for a factory, a *generic factory* interface is defined by the life cycle service in section 5.2.3. A generic factory is a creation service. It provides a generic operation for creation. Instead of invoking an object-specific operation on a factory with statically defined parameters, the client invokes a standard operation whose parameters can include information about resource filters, state initialization, policy preferences, etc.

To create an object, a client must possess an object reference for a factory, which may be either a generic factory or an object-specific factory, and issue an appropriate request on the factory. As a result, a new object is created and typically an object reference is returned.

There is nothing special about this interaction.

A factory assembles the resources necessary for the existence of an object it creates. Therefore, the factory represents a *scope* of resource allocation, which is the set of resources available to the factory. A factory may support an interface that enables its clients to *constrain* the scope.

Clients find factory objects in the same fashion they find any object. Two common scenarios for clients to find factories are:

- Clients use a finding mechanism, such as a naming context, drag-and-drop, or a trader, to find factories.
- Clients are passed factory objects as a parameter to an operation the client supports.

Various *implementation* strategies for factories are discussed in detail in section 5.3.

Client's Model of Deleting an Object

A client that wishes to delete an object issues a `remove`[1] request on an object supporting the *LifeCycleObject* interface. (The *LifeCycleObject* interface is defined in section 5.2.) The object receiving the request is called the *target.*

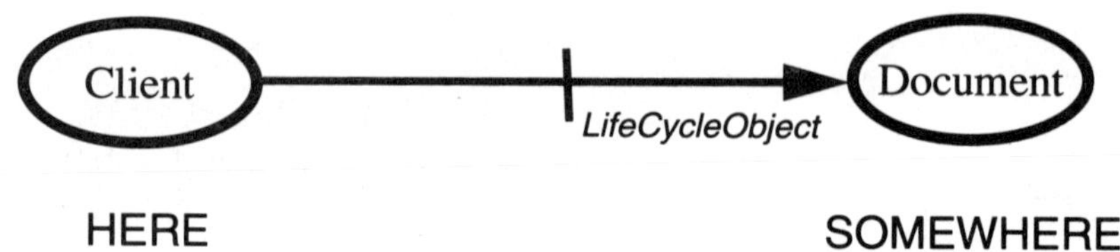

Figure 5-6 To delete an object, a client must posses an object reference supporting the *LifeCycleObject* interface and issues a `remove` request on the object.

Figure 5-6 illustrates a client deleting the document.

Client's Model of Copying or Moving an Object

A client that wishes to move or copy an object issues a `move` or `copy` request on an object supporting the *LifeCycleObject* interface. The object receiving the request is called the *target.*

The move and copy operations expect an object reference supporting the *FactoryFinder* interface. The factory finder represents the "THERE" in Figure 5-7. The client is indicating to move or copy the target using a factory within the scope of the factory finder. Section 5.1.4 describes factory finders in more detail.

1. The operation is named `remove`, rather than `delete`, because `delete` collides with the delete operator in C++.

The implementations of move and copy can use the factory finder to find appropriate factories "over there." Section 5.4 describes how objects can implement `move` and `copy` using the factory finder. This is invisible to the client.

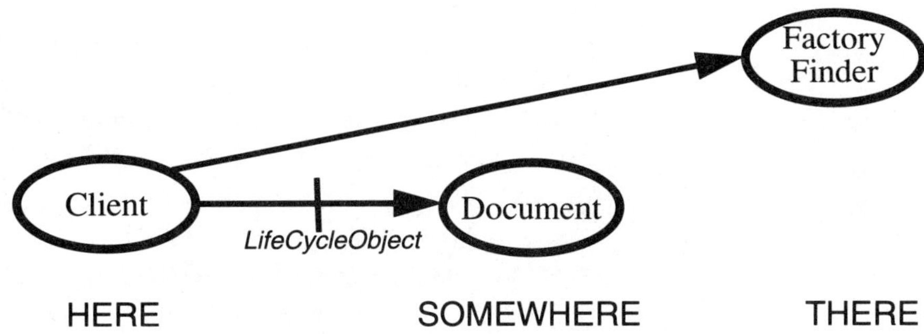

Figure 5-7 Life cycle services define how a client can move or copy an object from here to there.

In the example of Figure 5-7, client code would simply issue a `copy` request on the document and pass it an object supporting the *FactoryFinder* interface as an argument.

When a client issues a copy request on a target, it is assumed that the target, the factory finder, and the newly created object can all communicate via the ORB. With externalization/internalization there is no such assumption. In the presence of a future externalization service, the externalized form of the object can exist outside of the ORB for arbitrary amounts of time, be transported by means outside of the ORB and can be internalized in a different, disconnected ORB.

Note – In general, a client is unaware of how a target and a factory finder are implemented. The target may represent a simple object or it may represent a graph of objects. Similarly, a factory finder may represent a very concrete location, such as a specific storage device, or it may represent a more abstract location, such as a group of machines. The client uses the same interface in all of these cases.

5.1.4 *Factory Finders*

Factory finders support an operation, `find_factories`, which returns a sequence of factories. Clients pass factory finders to the move and copy operations, which typically invoke this operation to find a factory to interact with. (This is described in detail in section 5.4.) The new copy or the migrated object will then be within the scope of the factory finder.

Some examples of locations that a factory finder might represent are:

- somewhere on a work group's local area network
- storage device A on machine X
- Susan's notebook computer

Multiple Factory Finders

The factory finder interface given in section 5.2 represents the *minimal* functionality supported by all factory finders. Target implementations can depend on this operation being available. More sophisticated factory finding facilities can be provided by extended finding services.

Currently, the only finding service being considered for standardization by the OMG is the naming service. Others are likely to be standardized in the future. It is likely that there will always be multiple finding services, of different expressive powers, in distributed object systems.

As demonstrated in Figure 5-8, the *FactoryFinder* interface can be mixed in with interfaces for finding services, allowing multiple finding services. Many clients simply pass factory finders on to target objects. However, objects that need the services of a more powerful finding mechanism can narrow the factory finder to an appropriate, more specific interface.

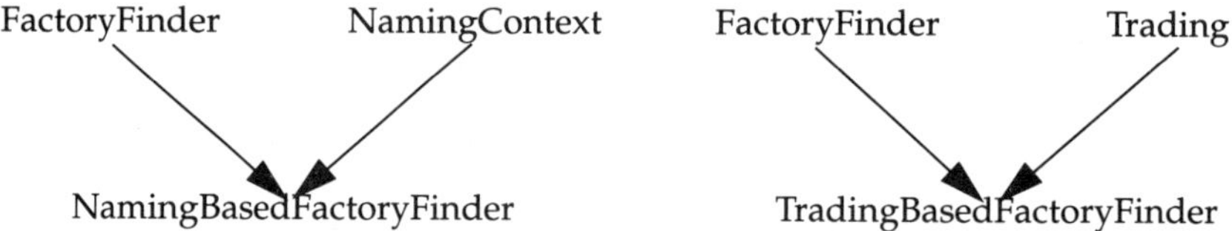

Figure 5-8 The *FactoryFinder* interface can be "mixed in" with interfaces of more powerful finding services.

The power of a factory finder is determined by the power of the finding service.

5.1.5 Design Principles

Several principles have driven the design of life cycle services:

1. A factory object registered at a factory finder represents an implementation at that location. Thus, a factory finder allows clients to query a location for an implementation.

2. Object implementations can embody knowledge of finding a factory, relative to a location. Object implementations usually do not embody knowledge of location.

3. The desired result for life cycle operations such as copy and move depends on relationships between the target object and other objects. The design given in appendix A has built-in support for the two most basic kinds of relationships, *containment* and *reference*, and supports the definition of new kinds of relationships and propagation semantics.
4. The life cycle service is not dependent on any particular model of persistence and is suitable for distributed, heterogeneous environments.
5. The design does not include an object equivalence service nor rely on global object identifiers.

5.1.6 Resolution of Technical Issues

This specification addresses the issues identified for life cycle services in the OMG *Object Services Architecture*[2] document as follows:

- *Creation*: Many of the parameters supplied to an object `create` operator will be implementation dependent, so that a standardized universal IDL signature for object creation is not possible. IDL signatures for object creation will be defined for various kinds of object factories, but the signatures will be specific to type, implementation, and persistent storage mechanism of the object to be created.
- *Deletion*: A `remove` operator is defined on any object supporting the *LifeCycleObject* interface. This model for deletion supports any desired paradigm for referential integrity. Appendix A describes support for the two most common paradigms, based on reference and containment relationships. Only one type of deletion is supported; a different operation should be used for archiving an object. This interface can support many paradigms for storage management (e.g., garbage collection and reference counts). Since storage management is implementation-dependent, its interface does not belong in the generalized life cycle interfaces.
- *Copying*: Appendix A describes support for shallow and deep copy, and referential integrity. A scheme based on reference and containment relationships defines scopes for operations such as copy. The concept of an *factory finder* is used for object location. This paradigm for copying, deleting, and moving objects works regardless of an object's ORB, persistent storage mechanism, and implementation. This design is extensible because objects participate in the traversal algorithm, and the relationship service presented in the appendix supports the definition of new kinds of relationships with different behavior.
- *Equivalence*: There was no need for an object equivalence service or global object identifiers in the design of the life cycle services to support real-world applications or other object services.

2. *Object Services Architecture*, Document Number 92-8-4, Object Managment Group, Framingham, MA, 1992.

5.2 The CosLifeCycle Module

Names of all IDC modules which form the Common Object Service Specification are prefixed with the initials "Cos."

Client code accesses the basic life cycle functionality via the *CosLifeCycle* module. This module defines the *FactoryFinder, LifeCycleObject* and *GenericFactory* interfaces and describes the operations of these interfaces in detail.

```
#include "Naming.idl"

module CosLifeCycle{

    typedef Naming::Name Key;
    typedef Object Factory;
    typedef sequence <Factory> Factories;
    typedef struct NVP {
        Naming::Istring name;
        any value;
    } NameValuePair;
    typedef sequence <NameValuePair> Criteria;

    exception NoFactory {
        Key search_key;
    };
    exception NotCopyable { string reason; };
    exception NotMovable { string reason; };
    exception NotRemovable { string reason; };
    exception InvalidCriteria{
        Criteria invalid_criteria;
    };
    exception CannotMeetCriteria {
        Criteria unmet_criteria;
    };

    interface FactoryFinder {
        Factories find_factories(in Key factory_key)
            raises(NoFactory);
    };

    interface LifeCycleObject {
        LifeCycleObject copy(in FactoryFinder there,
                in Criteria the_criteria)
            raises(NoFactory, NotCopyable, InvalidCriteria,
                 CannotMeetCriteria);
        void move(in FactoryFinder there,
                in Criteria the_criteria)
            raises(NoFactory, NotMovable, InvalidCriteria,
                 CannotMeetCriteria);
        void remove()
            raises(NotRemovable);
```

Figure 5-9 The `CosLifeCycle` module

```
    };

    interface GenericFactory {
        boolean supports(in Key k);
        Object create_object(
                in Key      k,
                in Criteria the_criteria)
            raises (NoFactory, InvalidCriteria,
                CannotMeetCriteria);
    };
};
```

Figure 5-9 The `CosLifeCycle` module *(continued)*

5.2.1 The LifeCycleObject Interface

The *LifeCycleObject* interface defines `copy`, `move` and `remove` operations. Objects participate in the life cycle service by supporting this interface.

copy

```
LifeCycleObject copy(in FactoryFinder there,
        in Criteria the_criteria)
    raises(NoFactory, NotCopyable, InvalidCriteria,
        CannotMeetCriteria);
```

The `copy` operation makes a copy of the object. The copy is located in the scope of the factory finder passed as the first parameter. The copy operation returns an object reference to the new object. The new object is initialized from the existing object.

The first parameter, `there`, may be a nil object reference. If passed a nil object reference, the target object can determine the location or fail with the `NoFactory` exception.

The second parameter, `the_criteria`, allows for a number of optional parameters to be passed. Typically, the target simply passes this parameter to the factory used in creating the new object. The criteria parameter is explained in detail in section 5.2.4

If the target cannot find an appropriate factory to create a copy "over there," the `NoFactory` exception is raised. An implementation that refuses to copy itself should raise the `NotCopyable` exception. If the target does not understand the criteria, the `InvalidCriteria` exception is raised. If the target understands the criteria but cannot satisfy the criteria, the `CannotMeetCriteria` exception is raised.

In addition to these exceptions, implementations may raise standard CORBA exceptions. For example, if resources cannot be acquired for the copied object, `NO_RESOURCES` will be raised. Similarly, if a target does not implement the copy operation, the `NO_IMPLEMENT` exception will be raised.

It is implementation dependent whether this operation is *atomic*.

move

```
void move(in FactoryFinder there,
        in Criteria the_criteria)
    raises(NoFactory, NotMovable, InvalidCriteria,
        CannotMeetCriteria);
```

The `move` operation on the target moves the object to the scope of the factory finder passed as the first parameter. The object reference for the target object remains valid after `move` has successfully executed.

The first parameter, `there`, may be a nil object reference. If passed a nil object reference, the target object can determine the location or fail with the `NoFactory` exception.

The second parameter, `the_criteria`, allows for a number of optional parameters to be passed. Typically, the target simply passes this parameter to the factory used in migrating the new object. The criteria parameter is explained in detail in section 5.2.4

If the target cannot find an appropriate factory to support migration of the object "over there," the `NoFactory` exception is raised. An implementation that refuses to move itself should raise the `NotMovable` exception. If the target does not understand the criteria, the `InvalidCriteria` exception is raised. If the target understands the criteria but cannot satisfy the criteria, the `CannotMeetCriteria` exception is raised.

In addition to these exceptions, implementations may raise standard CORBA exceptions. For example, if resources cannot be acquired for migrating the object, `NO_RESOURCES` will be raised. Similarly, if a target does not implement the move operation, the `NO_IMPLEMENT` exception will be raised.

It is implementation dependent whether this operation is *atomic*.

remove

```
void remove()
    raises(NotRemovable);
```

`Remove` instructs the object to cease to exist. The object reference for the target is no longer valid after remove successfully completes. The client is not responsible for cleaning up any resources the object uses. An implementation that refuses to remove itself should raise the `NotRemovable` exception. In addition to this exception, implementations may raise standard CORBA exceptions.

5.2.2 The FactoryFinder Interface

Factory finders support an operation, `find_factories`, which returns a sequence of factories. Clients pass factory finders to the move and copy operations, which typically invoke this operation to find a factory to interact with. (This is described in detail in section 5.4.)

The factory finder interface represents the *minimal* functionality supported by all factory finders.

find_factories

```
Factories find_factories(in Key factory_key)
    raises(NoFactory);
```

The `find_factories` operation is passed a key used to identify the desired factory. The key is a name, as defined by the naming service. More than one factory may match the key. As such, the factory finder returns a sequence of factories. If there are no matches, the `NoFactory` exception is raised.

The scope of the key is the factory finder. The factory finder assigns no semantics to the key. It simply matches keys. It makes no guarantees about the interface or implementation of the returned factories or objects they create.

It is beyond the scope of this specification to standardize the key space. The space of keys is established by *convention* in particular environments. The *kind* field[3] of the key is useful for partitioning the key space. *Suggested* values for the `id` and `kind` fields are given in Table 5-1.

Table 5-1 Suggested Conventions for Factory Finder Keys

id field	kind field	meaning
name of object interface	"object interface"	Find factories that create objects supporting the named interface.
name of equivalent implementations	"implementation equivalence class"	Find factories that create objects with implementations in a named equivalence class of implementations.*
name of object implementation	"object implementation"	Find factories that create objects of a particular implementation.
name of factory interface	"factory interface"	Find factories supporting the named factory interface.

* An example of an implementation equivalence class is a set of object implementations that have compatible externalized forms.

5.2.3 The GenericFactory Interface

In many environments, management of a set of resources that are allocated to objects at creation time is required. This needs to be done in a coordinated fashion for all types of objects. The LifeCycle Service provides a framework for this which is intended to be usable in a variety of administrative environments. However, the differing environments will administer a variety of resources and it is beyond the scope of this framework to identify all the possible types of resource.

While there is no standard interface for a factory, a *GenericFactory* interface is defined. The *GenericFactory* interface defines a generic creation operation, `create_object`. By defining a generic interface for creation, a creation service can be implemented. This is particularly useful in environments where administering a set of resources is important.

Such a generic factory can implement resource policies and represent multiple locations. In administered environments, object specific factories, such as the document factory described in section, may delegate the creation process to the generic factory. This is described in detail in section 5.3.2.

The job of the generic factory is to match the creation criteria specified by clients of the *GenericFactory* interface with offers made on behalf of implementation specific factories.

Figure 5-10 illustrates the structure of a creation service.

3. See the naming service specification.

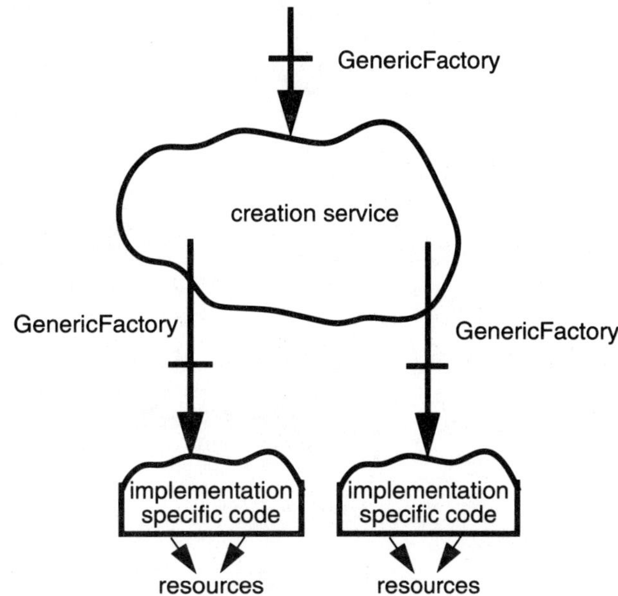

Figure 5-10 The life cycle service provides a generic creation capability. Ultimately, implementation-specific creation code is invoked by the creation service. The implementation-specific code also supports the *GenericFactory* interface.

The client of the *GenericFactory* interface invokes the `create_object` operation and can express criteria for creation.

Ultimately, this request will be passed to an implementation-specific factory which supports the *GenericFactory* interface. To get there, the request may travel through a number of generic factories. However, all of this is transparent to the client.

create_object

```
Object create_object(
        in Key k,
        in Criteria the_criteria)
    raises (NoFactory, InvalidCriteria,
        CannotMeetCriteria);
```

The `create_object` operation is passed a key used to identify the desired object to be created. The key is a name, as defined by the naming service.

The scope of the key is the generic factory. The generic factory assigns no semantics to the key. It simply matches keys. It makes no guarantees about the interface or implementation of the created object.

It is beyond the scope of this specification to standardize the key space. The space of keys is established by *convention* in particular environments. The *kind* field[4] of the key is useful for partitioning the key space. *Suggested* values for the id and kind fields are given in Table 5-2.

Table 5-2 Suggested Conventions for Generic Factory Keys

id field	kind field	meaning
name of object interface	"object interface"	Create an object that supports the named interface.
name of equivalent implementations	"implementation equivalence class"	Create an object whose implementation is in a named equivalence class of implementations.*
name of object implementation	"object implementation"	Create objects of a particular implementation.

* An example of an implementation equivalence class is a set of object implementations that have compatible externalized forms.

The second parameter, the_criteria, allows for a number of optional parameters to be passed. Criteria are explained in detail in section 5.2.4

If the generic factory cannot create an object specified by the key, then NoFactory is raised.

If the target does not understand the criteria, the InvalidCriteria exception is raised. If the target understands the criteria but cannot satisfy the criteria, the CannotMeetCriteria exception is raised.

supports

```
boolean supports(in Key k);
```

The supports operation returns true if the generic factory can create an object, given the key. Otherwise false is returned.

5.2.4 Criteria

The create_object operation of the *GenericFactory* interface expects a parameter specifying the creation criteria. The move and copy operations of the *LifeCycleObject* interface also expects this parameter; typically they pass it through to a factory. This section documents this parameter.

4. See the naming service specification.

The criteria parameter is expressed as an IDL sequence of name-value pairs. In particular, it is described by the following data structure given in the *CosLifeCycle* module:

```
typedef struct NVP {
    Naming::Istring name;
    any value;
} NameValuePair;
typedef sequence <NameValuePair> Criteria;
```

The parameter is given as a sequence of name-value pairs in order to be extensible and support "pass-through"; that is, new name-value pairs can be defined in the future and objects can be written that do not interpret the name-value pairs, but just pass them on to other objects.

Note – It is beyond the scope of this specification to standardize particular criteria. Supporting criteria is optional. Furthermore, supporting different criteria is acceptable. The criteria given here are *suggestions*.

Table 5-3 suggests criteria to be supported by the generic factory. Detailed descriptions follow.

Table 5-3 Suggested Criteria

criterion name	type of criterion value	interpretation
"initialization"	sequence<NameValuePair>	initialization parameters, given as a sequence of name-value pairs.
"filter"	string	allows clients of the generic factory to express a constraint on the created object.
"logical location"	sequence<NameValuePair>	allows clients of the generic factory to express a connection for the object, for example, a PCTE relationship.
"preferences"	string	a way for clients to influence the policies that a generic factory may use when creating an object

"initialization"

The "initialization" criterion is a sequence of name-value pairs which is intended to contain application-specific initialization values. Typically, the generic factory will pay no attention to the initialization criterion and simply passes it on to application specific factory code.

"filter"

The filter criterion is a constraint expression which provides the client with a powerful way of expressing its requirements on creation. The generic factory will use the constraint expression to make decisions about the allocation of particular resources. For example, a client could give a constraint "operating system" != "windows nt".

These constraints are expressed in some Constraint Language. A constraint language is suggested in Appendix 5B.

Filters are potentially complex and `InvalidCriteria` will be raised if the filter is too complex for the factory or is syntactically incorrect.

"logical location"

The "logical location" criterion allows a client to express where a created/copied/migrated object is logically created. For example, in PCTE an object is always in a relationship with another object. In such an environment, the logical location would specify another object and a relationship.

"preferences"

The "preferences" criterion allows the client to influence the policies which the generic factory uses to make decisions. For example, a generic factory might arbitrarily choose a machine from a set of machines. Using the preferences criterion, a client could express its preference for a particular machine. Policies and preferences are described in more detail in Appendix 5B.

5.3 Implementing Factories

As defined under Client's model of creation on page 68, any object that creates another object in response to some request is called a *factory*. Clients depend only on the definitions in that section.

The client's model of object life cycle has intentionally been defined abstractly. This allows a wide variety of implementation strategies.

Factories are *not* special objects. They have well-defined IDL interfaces and implementations in programming languages. Defining factory interfaces and implementing them are a normal part of application development.

Ultimately, the creation process requires implementation dependent code that assembles resources for the storage and execution of an object. The act of creating an object requires assembling and initializing all of the resources required to support the execution and storage of the object. The resources typically include:

- the allocation of one or more BOA object references, and
- resources related to persistence storage.

5.3.1 Minimal Factories

Figure 5-11 illustrates a minimal implementation of a factory that assembles resources in a single factory object.

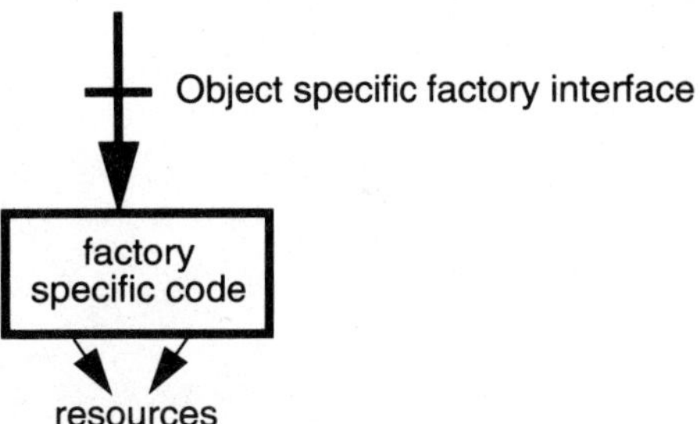

Figure 5-11 Factories assemble resources for the execution of an object. A minimal implementation achieves this with a single factory implementation.

5.3.2 Administered Factories

Factories can delegate the creation process to a generic factory that administers a set of resources. The generic factory may apply policies to all creation requests.

Eventually, such a generic creation service needs to communicate with implementation-specific code that actually assembles the resources for the object. Figure 5-12 illustrates an object-specific factory, such as the document factory of Figure 5-5 that delegates the creation problem to the generic creation service. The object-specific factory effectively adds a statically typed wrapper around the generic factory.

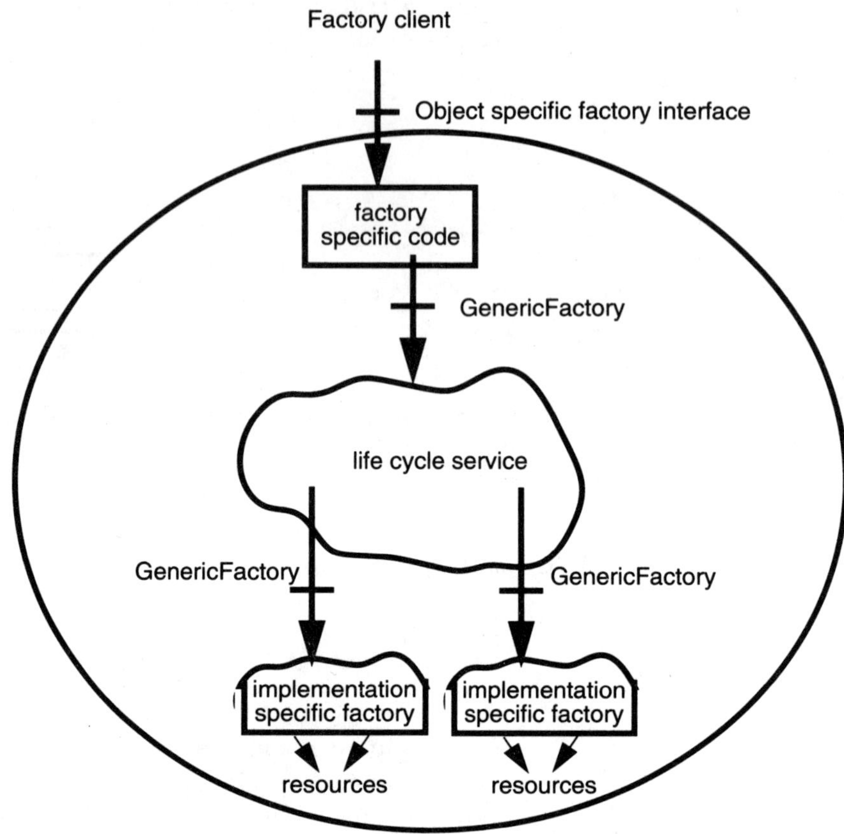

Figure 5-12 In an administered environment, factory *implementations* can delegate the creation problem to a generic factory. The generic factory can apply resource allocation policies. Ultimately the creation service communicates with implementation specific code that assembles resources for the object.

5.4 Target's Use of Factories and Factory Finders

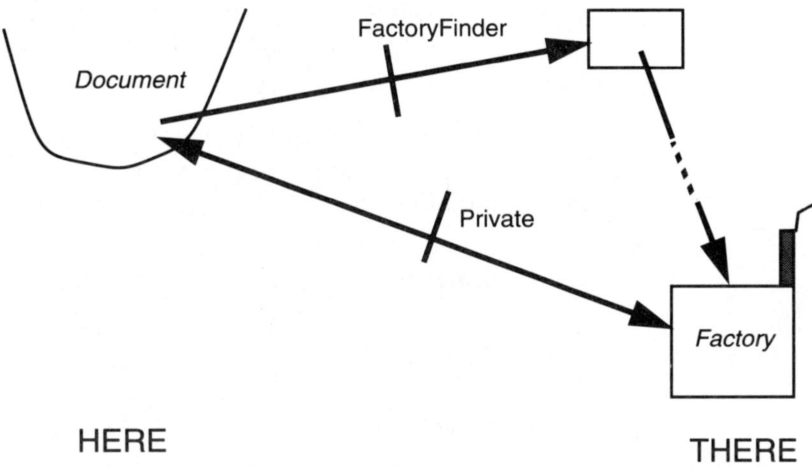

Figure 5-13 The copy and move operations are passed a *FactoryFinder* to represent "there." The implementation of the target uses the *FactoryFinder* to find a factory object for creation over there. The protocol between the object and the factory is private. They can communicate and transfer state according to any implementation-defined protocol.

A client passes a factory finder as a parameter to a copy or move request.

Clients do not generally understand the *implementation* constraints of the object being copied. Clients cannot express what the target object needs in order to copy itself to the new location.

Target object implementations, on the other hand, put constraints on factories based on implementation concerns. It is unlikely that target implementation code is interested in further constraining location.

To find an appropriate factory, the target object implementation may use the factory finder with its minimal interface defined in section 5.2.2 or it may attempt to narrow the factory finder to a more sophisticated finding service with more expressive power. The target object implementation can always depend on the existence of the minimal interface.

Once the target object implementation finds a factory, it communicates with the factory using a *private*, implementation-defined, interface.

5.5 Summary of Life Cycle Services

The problem of distributed object life cycle is

- the problem of creating an object,

- the problem of deleting an object,
- the problem of moving and copying an object and
- the problem of operating on a graph of distributed objects.

The client's model of object life cycle is based on *factories* and target objects supporting the *LifeCycleObject* interface. Factories are objects that create other objects. The *LifeCycleObject* interface defines operations to delete an object, to move an object and to copy an object.

A *GenericFactory* interface is defined. The generic factory interface is sufficient to create objects of different types. By defining a *GenericFactory* interface, implementations that administer resources are enabled.

To summarize:

The life cycle service specification includes:

- The *LifeCycleObject* interface
- The *FactoryFinder* interface
- The *GenericFactory* interface

The appendices that follow are not part of the life cycle specification. They are included as background material. Appendix 5A discusses how the *LifeCycleObject* interface can be supported for graphs of distributed objects using a relationship service. Appendix 5B suggests a filtering language for the filter criteria. Appendix 5C discusses administration of generic factories. Appendix 5D discusses support for PCTE objects.

Appendix 5A Life Cycle Operations on Graphs of Distributed Objects

Note – Appendix 5A is not part of the Life Cycle Services specification. It sketches how the life cycle services, a hypthesized future relationship service, and a hypothesized future externalization service might play together to support graphs of distributed objects. This description is included here for several reasons:

- Distributed objects do not *float* in space. They are connected to other objects. Performing life cycle operations on an object affects other objects. This appendix describes how life cycle operations can be supported for graphs of distributed objects.
- This approach to graphs of distributed objects demonstrates that so-called "shallow" and "deep" operations are not well-defined notions.
- Externalization will be defined in future OMG specifications. This appendix describes how those operations fit.

The connections between objects in a graph are called *relationships*. Relationships allow semantics to be added to references between objects. For example, associations allow one object to *contain* another. Life Cycle services must work in the presence of graphs of related objects.

As described in section 5.1.3, a client issues a life cycle request on a *target* object. A target implements the target operations as appropriate. If the target represents a simple object, that is, an object that is not part of a graph of associated objects, the target should provide an implementation for each of the operations in the *LifeCycleObject* interface described in section 5.2.1.

5A.1 The Traversal Service

If the target represents an object that is a node in a graph of distributed objects, life cycle services defines a *traversal object* to support the orderly operation on the graph. This section defines the traversal object and focuses on its use by a target implementation.

In response to one of the requests defined in the *LifeCycleObject* interface, a target object simply creates a traversal object and issues a life cycle request on it. The traversal object supports analogous move, copy, remove, externalize and internalize operations on the graph.

The operations on the traversal object expect a *Node* object reference as a starting node. The *Node* interface defines what a node in the graph of associated objects must support in order to participate in the graph of associated objects. The target passes its *Node* object reference to the traversal service.

Figure 5A-1 graphically illustrates the target's view of the traversal object.

The traversal object operates on the nodes of the graph. The traversal object and the associates cooperate to maintain the integrity of the graph.

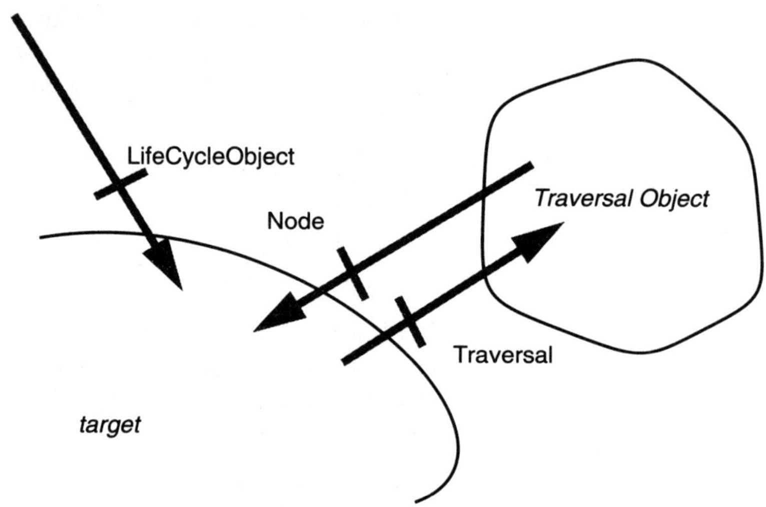

Figure 5A-1 A target that is part of a graph of associated objects can implement a life cycle operation by creating a traversal object and issuing a request on the traversal object. The target passes to the traversal object an object reference that supports the *Node* interface.

5A.2 A Node's View of Life Cycle Services

Recall that a client issues a life cycle request on a target object. A target object that is part of a *graph of associated objects* creates a traversal object to operate on the graph. The traversal object operates on the nodes of the graph.

A node cooperates with the traversal object. Figure 5A-2 illustrates the node's view of the life cycle services. A node in the graph supports the *Node* interface. The *Node* interface defines operations to copy, move, remove and externalize the node.

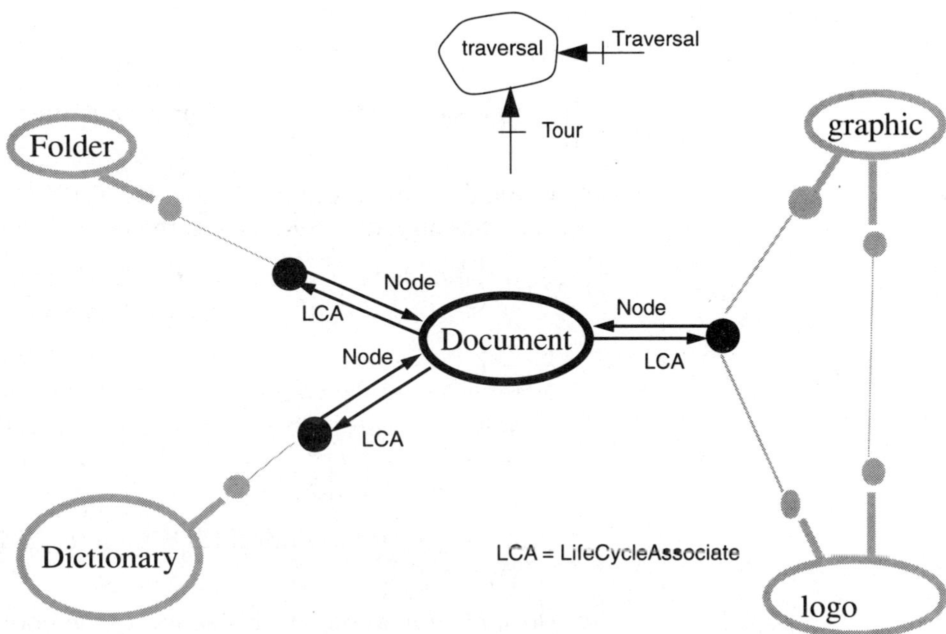

Figure 5A-2 A node in a graph of associated objects

The traversal object passes a *Tour* object to a node. Through the tour object, nodes and traversals exchange identifiers. This allows nodes and traversals to identify each other during the life of the traversal. This exchange of identifiers allows:

- a node to distinguish multiple concurrent life cycle operations and
- a traversal object to recognize a node it has already visited.

The node has a set of associates that represent its participation in relationships with other objects. For example, one associate may represent the objects it *contains*. Another associate may represent the objects it *references*. When the traversal object performs a life cycle operation on the node, the node performs the operation on itself and on its associates. The associates support the *LifeCycleAssociate* interface. The *LifeCycleAssociate* interface defines operations to copy, move, remove and externalize the associate.

Through the operations of the *Node* interface, the node reveals its associates to the traversal object. The traversal object asks the associates for their connections to other associates. Based on these connections, the traversal object operates on other nodes.

To summarize a node's view of the life cycle protocols:

- a node *supports* the *Node* interface,
- a node *uses* the *Tour* interface to exchange identifiers with the traversal object and
- a node *uses* the *LifeCycleAssociate* interface to operate on its associates.

5A.3 Traversal Algorithms

The implementations of the traversal operations typically have the following structure:

- While there are more nodes to visit, apply the operation to a node. If the node has already been visited, the node is skipped.
  a. If the node has not yet been visited, the result is a set of associates supporting the *LifeCycleAssociate* interface.
  b. Ask the associates what to do for the particular operation. The associate replies with the *propagation* attribute for the operation. For example, if the associate represents the *contains* role of containment, the associate would reply that copy *propagates* to the contained objects. Propagation is defined in detail in section 5A.4.
  c. If the operation propagates to another node, add it to a list of nodes to visit.
- Do some operation-specific action to the nodes and edges that have been visited. For example, the copy operation links new associates together.

The key to this interaction is the interface used by the traversal object to communicate with the associates.

5A.4 Containment and Reference

The edges in the graph represent the relationships between the objects. Two *common* relationships are *containment* and *reference*. Containment is a one-to-many relationship. A container can contain many containees; a containee is contained by one container. Reference, on the other hand, is a many-to-many relationship. An object can reference many objects; an object can be referenced by many objects.

Containment and reference are *examples* of relationships. The relationship service allows application developers to define new kinds of relationships. Since containment and reference are very common relationships, this appendix will explore them further and define *propagation semantics* for containment and reference. In doing so it will define the behavior of copy, move, remove and externalize in the presence of containment and reference.

ContainsAssociate, ContainedInAssociate, ReferencesAssociate and ReferencedByAssociate are defined as subtypes of *LifeCycleAssociate.* Figure 5A-3 illustrates a document that references a phone book and a dictionary and contains a graphic and a logo.

The traversal object depends only on the *LifeCycleAssociate* interface and not on these particular relationships.

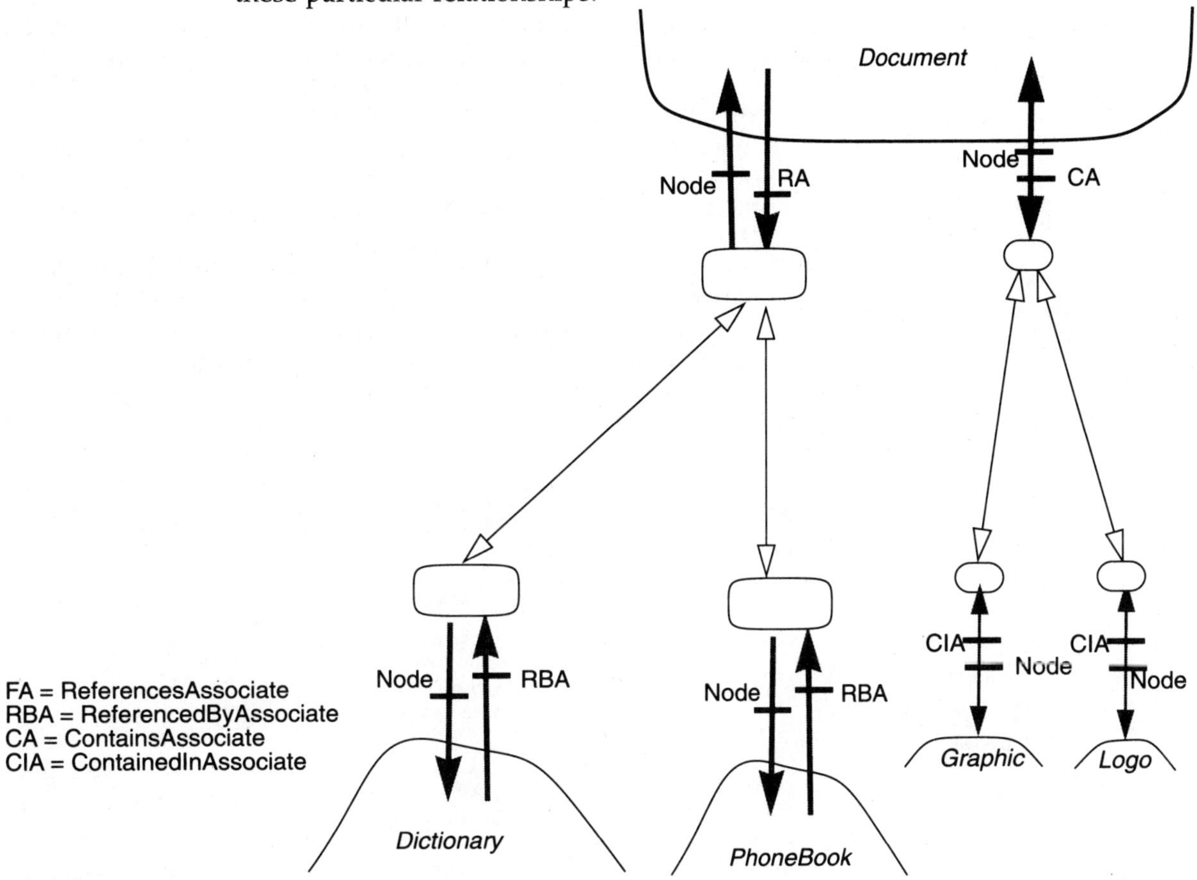

Document
Node
RA
Node
CA
FA = ReferencesAssociate
RBA = ReferencedByAssociate
CA = ContainsAssociate
CIA = ContainedInAssociate
Node
RBA
Node
RBA
CIA
Node
CIA
Node
Graphic
Logo
Dictionary
PhoneBook

Figure 5A-3 A document that references a phone book and a dictionary and contains a graphic and a logo

Life Cycle Propagation Across Associates

This section defines how the life cycle operations affect the containment and reference relationships. The traversal object applies a life cycle operation to a node in the graph and then queries the associates for their propagation behavior. Table 5A-1 and Table 5A-2 indicate the behavior of the life cycle operation from an associate to the corresponding associate. The behavior is given by one of three attributes:

- deep
- shallow
- none

Deep means that the operation is applied to the associates and to the associated objects. For example, when copying a document that *contains* a graphic, the copy propagates to the graphic. The traversal object copies the document, the graphic and establishes a new containment relationship between the copies.

Shallow means that the operation is applied to the relationship but not to the associated objects. For example, removing a graphic contained in a document, removes the graphic, removes the containment relationship between the graphic and the document but does not remove the document.

None means that the operation has no effect on the relationship and no effect on the related objects. For example, copying an object that is referenced by another copies the object but has no effect on the object that refers to it or on the reference relationship.

Table 5A-1 Containment

operation	**ContainsAssociate**	**ContainedInAssociate**
copy	deep	shallow
move	deep	shallow
remove	deep	shallow
externalize	deep	none

Table 5A-2 Reference

operation	**ReferencesAssociate**	**ReferencedByAssociate**
copy	shallow	none
move	shallow	shallow
remove	shallow	shallow
externalize	none	none

The propagation attributes are available from the associates using an operation in the *LifeCycleAssociate* interface. A *ContainsAssociate* returns the values of the first column of Table 5A-1. A *ContainedInAssociate* returns the values of the second column of Table 5A-1. A *ReferencesAssociate* returns the values of the first column of Table 5A-2. A *ReferencedByAssociate* returns the values of the second column of Table 5A-2.

A designer of a new relationship needs to define the propagation behavior for the associates. An implementation of a traversal object needs to operate according to the propagation values defined by the associate.

5A.5 Notes

1. The model of operation propagation across associates is derived from [1.]. See that paper for a thorough discussion.
2. When propagating a copy to an object that participates in relationships with different propagation semantics, it is possible that copy *propagates* to object by one relationship and that copy is *shallow* by another relationship. In such a case, shallow is *promoted* to propagate by the traversal object.
3. Shallow is meaningless for externalize. Externalize should produce a "self-contained graph." Implementations of externalize can externalize *names* for objects outside of the graph. *Internalize* can then resolve those names in the new environment.

5A.6 References

1. James Rumbaugh, "Controlling Propagation of Operations using Attributes on Relations," *OOPSLA 1988 Proceedings*, p. 285–296
2. Rick Cattell, *Object Data Management*, Reading, Mass., Addison Wesley, 1991.
3. OMG, "The Common Object Request Broker: Architecture and Specification," OMG Document Number 91.12.1, December 1991.

Appendix 5B Filters

Note – Appendix 5B is not part of the Life Cycle Services specification. It sketches a mechanism for expressing filters. This appendix is included to provided an example of how a filter might be provided.

A factory represents a scope of resource allocation, which is the set of resources available to the factory. Whenever it receives a creation request, a factory will allocate resources according to any policies which are in operation.

Clearly, by choosing a particular factory upon which to issue a create request, a client is exerting some control over the allocation of resources. Therefore, a client can limit the scope of resource allocation, by issuing the request on a different factory which represents a smaller set of resources.

However, there are two problems with this. First, the granularity of resources may be much smaller than the granularity represented by the factories in a system. For example, there are unlikely to be factories which represent individual disk segments.

Second, the client may wish to rule out the use of particular resources within a scope, but avoid having a general reduction in scope. For example, the client might not be concerned with which machine within a LAN an object is created on, providing it is not on machine X.

Both of these needs can be addressed by providing a filter. In the first case, the filter is relatively simple; it will simply limit the scope of resource allocation. In the second case, the filter will need to be more sophisticated.

This appendix describes one way of providing filters using *properties* and *constraint expressions*. These concepts appear in the development of Trading in the ISO/IEC/CCITT Open Distributed Processing standards. Service providers register their service with the Trader and use properties to describe the service offer. Potential clients may then use constraint expressions to describe the requirements which service offers must satisfy.

Similarly, the life cycle service may define a number of properties to represent the different kinds of resources available within in a system and clients may use constraint expressions to place the restrictions upon the use of those resources.

Note – The Object Services Architecture identifies an Object Properties Service which enables an object to have a set of arbitrary named values associated with it. These are very similar to the concept of properties as used in Trading and in this appendix.

5B.1 Resources as Properties

Resource properties are application and generic factory implementation dependent and it is beyond the scope of this specification to identify standard properties which all generic factory implementations will recognize. The properties described in this appendix are given as examples only. Table 5B-1 gives some examples of properties that might be supported by a generic factory.

Table 5B-1 Examples of Properties Supported by a Generic Factory

Property Name	Meaning
Host	Host name of the machine
Architecture	Machine architecture, e.g., "intel," "sparc"
OSArchitecture	Operating system architecture, e.g., "solaris," "hpux"

5B.2 Constraint Expressions

Constraints are expressed in a Constraint Language which provides a set of operators which allow arbitrarily complex expressions involving properties and potential values to be specified. A property lists *satisfies* a constraint if the constraint expression is true when evaluated with respect to the property list.

Constraint expressions are very flexible. For example, if a client has an object executing on a machine called 'Host1' and wishes to create another object which is *not* on the same machine, the client can specify the constraint "Host != 'Host1'".

The constraint expression described here works with properties for which the value can be a string, a number, or a set of values.

The constraint language consists of:

- comparative functions: `==`, `!=`, `>`, `>=`, `<`, `<=`, `in`
- constructors: `and`, `or`, `not`
- property names
- numeric and string constants
- mathematical operators: `+`, `-`, `*`, `/`
- grouping operators: `(`, `)`, `[`, `]`

The following precedence relations hold in the absence of parentheses, in the order of lowest to highest:

- `+` and `-`
- `*` and `/`
- `or`
- `and`
- `not`

The comparative operator `in` checks for the inclusion of a particular string constant in the list which is the value of a property.

5B.3 BNF for Constraint Expressions

```
<ConstraintExpr>    :=    [ <Expr> ]

<Expr>              :=    <Expr> "or" <Expr>
                    |     <Expr> "and" <Expr>
                    |     "not" <Expr>
                    |     "(" <Expr> ")"
                    |     <SetExpr> <SetOp> <SetExpr>
                    |     <StrExpr> <StrOp> <StrExpr>
                    |     <NumExpr> <NumOp> <NumExpr>
                    |     <NumExpr> "in" <SetExpr>
                    |     <StrExpr> "in" <SetExpr>

<NumOp>             :=    "==" | "!=" | "<" | "<=" | ">" | ">="

<StrOp>             :=    "==" | "!="

<SetOp>             :=    "==" | "!="

<NumExpr>           :=    <NumTerm>
                    |     <NumExpr> "+" <NumTerm>
                    |     <NumExpr> "-" <NumTerm>

<NumTerm>           :=    <NumFactor>
                    |     <NumTerm> "*" <NumFactor>
                    |     <NumTerm> "/" <NumFactor>

<NumFactor>         :=    <Identifier>
                    |     <Number>
                    |     "(" <NumExpr> ")"
                    |     "-" <NumFactor>

<StrExpr>           :=    <StrTerm>
                    |     <StrExpr> "+" <StrTerm>

<StrTerm>           :=    <Identifier>
                    |     <String>
                    |     "(" <StrExpr> ")"

<SetExpr>           :=    <SetTerm>
                    |     <SetExpr> "+" <SetTerm>

<SetTerm>           :=    <Identifier>
                    |     <Set>
                    |     "(" <SetExpr> ")"

<Identifier>        :=    <Word>
```

```
<Number>        :=   <Integer>
                |    <Float>

<Integer>       :=   { <Digit> }+

<Float>         :=   <Mantissa> [ <Sign> ] [ <Exponent> ]

<Mantissa>      :=   <Integer> [ "." [ <Integer> ] ]
                |    "." <Integer>

<Sign>          :=   "-"
                |    "+"

<Exponent>      :=   "e" <Integer>
                |    "E" <Integer>

<Word>          :=   <Letter> { <AlphaNum> }*

<AlphaNum>      :=   <Letter>
                |    <Digit>
                |    "_"

<String>        :=   "'" { <Char> }* "'"

<Char>          :=   <Letter>
                |    <Digit>
                |    <Other>

<Set>           :=   "{" <Elements> "}"

<Elements>      :=   [ <Element> { <Sp>+ <Element> }* ]

<Element>       :=   <Number>
                |    <Word>
                |    <String>

<Letter>        :=   a | b | c | d | e | f | g | h | i | j | k
                |    l | m | n | o | p | q | r | s | t | u | v
                |    w | x | y | z | A | B | C | D | E | F | G
                |    H | I | J | K | L | M | N | O | P | Q | R
                |    S | T | U | V | W | X | Y | Z

<Digit>         :=   0 | 1 | 2 | 3 | 4 | 5 | 6 | 7 | 8 | 9

<Other>         :=   <Sp> | ~ | ! | @ | # | $ | % | ^ | & | * | (
                |    ) | - | _ | = | + | [ | { | ] | } | ; | :
                |    " | \ | | | , | < | . | > | / | ?

<Sp>            :=   " "
```

Appendix 5C Administration

Note – Appendix 5C is not part of the Life Cycle Services specification. This description is included as a suggested way of administering generic factories.

The specification for the life cycle service includes the *GenericFactory* interface. There will be at least two styles of object which support that interface:

- implementation specific factories that actually assemble the resources for a new object, and
- generic factories which pass requests on to either implementation-specific factories or other generic factories.

By configuring generic factories and implementation-specific factories into a graph, a creation service can be built which administers the allocation of a large number of resources and can use them to create a wide variety of objects.

To ensure that the creation service is scalable, it is essential that the principle of *federation* is adopted—each component retains its autonomy rather than becoming subordinate to another.

Whenever the creation service receives a creation request, the request will need to traverse the graph until it reaches an implementation specific factory which can satisfy the request. As the request traverses the graph, each nonterminal node in the graph (i.e., the generic factories) will decide which link the request will traverse next. Decisions will be based upon information about each available link, any *policies* in force at that node and, of course, the actual request.

Clearly, the configuration and policies of such a creation service will need to be administered. However, the specification does not include the specification of an administration interface. This is because the principle of federation is not only important to the life cycle service. It will be essential to a number of other services, notably trading, and the OMG plans to address the issue of federation for *all* object services, rather than making a premature specification addressing the needs of just one service.

The remainder of this appendix describes the principle of federation in more detail, outlines the use of policies and preferences to support federation, and then concludes with a suggestion for how an administration interface might look.

5C.1 Federation

Federation is essential in large-scale distributed systems where the existence of centralized ownership and universal control cannot be assumed. In these systems the only way to achieve cooperation between autonomous systems without creating a hierarchical structure is to use federation. Federation is also beneficial to smaller systems which can exploit the high degree of flexibility which federation provides.

Federation differs from the more conventional approach of adopting a strictly hierarchical organization in a number of ways. First, components can provide their service to any number of others, not just the single component which is its "parent" in the hierarchy. Second, components can establish peer-to-peer relationships, eliminating the need for a single component at the top of the hierarchy. Finally, this approach avoids the necessity of maintaining a global namespace. Instead, all names are relative to the context in which they are used.

Federation enables previously distinct systems to be unified without requiring global changes to their naming structures and system management hierarchies. The administration functions must ensure the systems are configured appropriately (e.g., avoiding circular references in those graphs which must be kept acyclic).

5C.1.1 Federation in OMG Object Services

In addition to the use of federation in configuring generic factories, federation is also applicable to a number of other services.

Trading is a notable example. A global offer space is neither practical nor desirable. Consequently, there will be multiple traders, each representing a different portion of the offer space. Offers held by one trader can be made available to the clients of another trader through federation.

The naming service specification also demonstrates attributes of federation. Naming contexts can be bound to other naming contexts and requests for name resolution can be passed across the links. However, it is entirely the concern of the naming context how it resolves the name within its domain (i.e., it is autonomous).

5C.1.2 Federation Issues

There are a number of issues which need to be addressed for federation to be used in a cohesive fashion across all object services.

Visibility of the Federation Graph

The naming service makes the configuration of naming contexts into a graph very visible to the clients. This is essential, because the naming service must provide clients with a structured namespace.

On the other hand, it is not clear that a client should ever be able to see the internal structure of a life cycle creation service built with generic and implementation-specific factories.

The trading service falls in between the two extremes. It may be useful for a client to be able to navigate the structure of a trading service graph in order to have more control over the visibility of offers. However, this may make clients too dependent upon the organization of the trading service and limit the flexibility of the system administrator in reorganizing the trading service to provide the most effective service.

Service Interface vs. Administration Interface

In general, it is desirable to federate using the service interface for the links and reserve the administration interface for the administrators. This approach ensures that autonomy is retained. However, this precludes the use of compound names in the administration functions because the administration functions cannot traverse the graph; only simple names can be used in administration-only functions.

However, this is inappropriate for services where graph manipulation is an essential part of the service. For example, the naming service specification does not distinguish between administration functions for manipulating the graph and service functions. This is clearly correct; the clients need to be able to manipulate the graph by creating, binding and destroying contexts.

Multiple Service Interfaces

A node in a federation graph may be a conspiracy and offer multiple service interfaces, perhaps one for each point it is bound into the graph. However, for services where the administration is kept distinct from the service, it is likely that the conspiracy will support only one administration interface.

In these situations, it becomes necessary for an administrator to be able to match service interfaces to conspiracies (i.e., to match one or more service interfaces to an administrative interface). The example in Section 5C.3 provides a solution to this which, in theory, will scale, but there may be better ways of doing this.

Cycles and Peer-to-Peer Relationships

The introduction of cycles into a federation graph is a contentious issue. Since peer-to-peer relationships are a degenerate form of cycle, any service which supports peer-to-peer relationships must be capable of handling cycles. The major impact of this is to provide loop detection on operations which would otherwise go out of control. Both trading and naming services are examples of this kind of service.

However, some services may not be able to handle cycles effectively and will wish to proscibe them. This probably covers peer-to-peer relationships, although that might be an acceptable special case. An example of this might be the life cycle creation service, where information about the current usage of the available resources must percolate up the graph in order to make informed decisions, but the introduction of cycles would make this information unclear or even meaningless.

5C.2 Policies

It is frequently necessary to configure the way in which operations are performed in order to tune the performance (e.g., how long a search operation may take, how many matches can be returned, or how much memory to use for a cache).

The same problems exist in distributed systems except that such configuration parameters must be explicitly passed around. Where different administrative domains are connected, such configuration parameters cannot be enforced by one domain on the other. Similarly, users may want to control the configuration but must be prevented from hogging resources (e.g., memory, disk space, etc.). Some configuration elements must be enforced (e.g., disk quotas), some elements may specify defaults which can be changed and some elements may be requests which may or may not clash with hard limits (e.g., max memory per process).

Policies are used as a generic solution to this problem—wherever some kind of choice needs to be made, policies may be used to guide the decision-making process.

Table 5C-1 provides some examples of policies which a federated service might support.

Table 5C-1 Example Policies

Policy Name	Meaning
search_algorithm	determines whether the federation graph should be traversed in a depth first or breadth first fashion.
cross_ boundaries	determines whether administrative boundaries should be crossed.
maximum_distance	how far to traverse a graph before failing a request.

When invoking operations, clients can specify preferences for particular policies. Providing the service has no value set for that policy, the preference will be simply added to the policy list for the duration of the request. However, if a service policy is already specified then the preference will either be ignored or, for policies such as "maximum_distance", the more constraining value will be adopted.

As a request traverses a graph, each node will pass its current policy set as preferences. In this way, the autonomy of individual administrative domains is preserved.

When an object doesn't implement all choices of a policy, it should not allow its policy to be modified to an unsupported value. This means that implementation limitations are handled as Administrative hard limits which provides the correct semantics.

Where no policy is specified by either administrator or client, the implementation determines its own behavior. However, this decision would not be propagated through the graph (as a preference), leaving it to each node in the graph to make its own decision.

5C.3 An Example LifeCycleService Module

Administrators access the administration functions via the *LifeCycleService* module, which defines the *LifeCycleServiceAdmin* interface. This example is intended to work with the *GenericFactory* interface in the specification. As a result, the administration functions cannot make use of compound names.

```
#include "LifeCycle.idl"

module LifeCycleService {

    typedef sequence <Lifecycle::NameValuePair> PolicyList;
    typedef sequence <Lifecycle::Key> Keys;
    typedef sequence <Lifecycle::NameValuePair> PropertyList;
    typedef sequence <Naming::NameComponent> NameComponents;

    interface LifeCycleServiceAdmin {

        attribute PolicyList policies;

        void bind_generic_factory(
                in Lifecycle::GenericFactory gf,
                in Naming::NameComponent name,
                in Keys key_set,
                in PropertyList other_properties)
            raises (Naming::AlreadBound, Naming::InvalidName);

        void unbind_generic_factory(
                in Naming::NameComponent name)
            raises (Naming::NotFound, Naming::InvalidName);

        Lifecycle::GenericFactory resolve_generic_factory(
                in Naming::NameComponent name)
            raises (Naming::NotFound, Naming::InvalidName);
```

Figure 5C-1 The `LifeCycleService` module

```
        NameComponents list_generic_factories();

        boolean match_service (in Lifecycle::GenericFactory f);

        string get_hint();

        void get_link_properties(
                in Naming::NameComponent name,
                out Keys key_set,
                out PropertyList other_properties)
            raises (Naming::NotFound, Naming::InvalidName);
    };

};
```

Figure 5C-1 The `LifeCycleService` module *(continued)*

5C.3.1 *The LifeCycleServiceAdmin Interface*

The *LifeCycleServiceAdmin* interface provides the basic administration operations required to enable the lifecycle service to be administered by a set of tools or an administration service. The operations enable configuration of factories supporting the *GenericFactory* interface into a graph and setting of policies for those factories.

bind_generic_factory

```
    void bind_generic_factory(
            in Lifecycle::GenericFactory gf,
            in Naming::NameComponent name,
            in Keys key_set,
            in PropertyList other_properties)
        raises (Naming::AlreadBound, Naming::InvalidName);
```

This operation binds a factory supporting the *GenericFactory* interface into a graph. The `name` must be unique within the context of the target of the operation. From then on, that factory can be identified by that name.

In order to make a good decision about which link to choose for a request, the node needs to be provided with additional information about those factories. This information may be fairly dynamic (e.g., the current usage of the resources available through the link), or more static (e.g., the Keys for which the link can provide support).

The `key_set` parameter is a list of the keys for which the factory can provide support. In the case of an implementation-specific factory, this list will often only have one member.

The `other_properties` parameter can be used to provide other static properties associated with the factory. For example, an "Architectures" property would indicate the type(s) of machine which the factory could create objects on.

Changes to the static information as well as more dynamic information can be monitored through the Events service. Each factory would generate events whenever the information changed significantly (e.g., a new *GenericFactory* interface with new keys is bound to the factory, or there is a change in the usage of resources available to the factory) and these can then be passed to those factories which need to know.

unbind_generic_factory

```
void unbind_generic_factory(
        in Naming::NameComponent name)
    raises (Naming::NotFound, Naming::InvalidName);
```

This operation unbinds the generic factory identified by the name.

resolve_generic_factory

```
Lifecycle::GenericFactory resolve_generic_factory(
        in Naming::NameComponent name)
    raises (Naming::NotFound, Naming::InvalidName);
```

This operation takes the name supplied and returns the reference to the *GenericFactory* object.

list_generic_factories

```
NameComponents list_generic_factories();
```

This operation returns a list of the names of all the bound factories.

match_service

```
boolean match_service (in Lifecycle::GenericFactory f);
```

This operation returns `true` if the generic factory interface is supported by the target.

get_hint

```
string get_hint();
```

This operation returns a hint associated with the target; see *Building a Map of a Graph* below.

get_link_properties

```
void get_link_properties(
        in Naming::NameComponent name,
        out Keys key_set,
        out PropertyList other_properties)
    raises (Naming::NotFound, Naming::InvalidName);
```

This operation returns the `key_set` and `other_properties` associated with the `name`.

Building a Map of a Graph

Administration tools may wish to build a map of a federation graph from scratch and some of the operations above are provided for that purpose.

First of all, the tool must obtain the set of administration interfaces for all the factories to be administered. These might be obtained from a number of sources (e.g., a well-known trading context).

For each interface, the `list_generic_factories` operation obtains a list of all the links for each node. Using `resolve_generic_factory`, a service interface can be obtained for each link. These can then be matched to an administration interface using `match_service`.

Clearly, this does not scale well if there are many nodes involved because of the average number of invocations of `match_service` required. This problem can be solved if one of the `other_properties` associated with each service interface is a *hint* and a hint is available for each administration interface. If the hints are the same, there may be a match and `match_service` is called to check. If the hints could be guaranteed to be unambiguous, the invocation could be avoided altogether, but this requires a global namespace for the hints. The best that can reasonably be achieved is to reduce the chance of a clash to a minimum.

The `get_hint` and `get_link_properties` can be used for this purpose.

Appendix 5D Support for PCTE Objects[1]

Note – Appendix 5D is not part of the Life Cycle Services specification. This appendix defines a set of criteria[2] suitable for supporting PCTE objects.

It is intended that objects in a PCTE repository be among those objects that can be managed though this life cycle interface. It is reasonable to expect that applications written for PCTE will use the PCTE APIs to manage the life cycle of PCTE objects. It is also reasonable to expect that clients not specifically written for relationship-oriented objects will not be able to manipulate the life cycles of PCTE objects. However, between these two, one can envision clients which desire to be flexible, working on objects which may or may not be stored in the PCTE repository. One can also envision object factories, constructed to make use of PCTE, which provide services to clients that are not PCTE applications because they do not have the appropriate working schemas, etc.

Support for these clients employs a series of conventional interpretations of the life cycle operations. This appendix provides one such set of conventions to demonstrate the feasibility of the use of these interfaces in a context supporting PCTE.

Object references appear in constraint expressions in the form of character strings. Any implementation of PCTE as a CORBA Object Adapter has to establish a relationship between these and the corresponding CORBA types, and be able to convert between them.

5D.1 Overview

A PCTE repository can be viewed as a generic factory. Using whatever naming or trading services are appropriate, a client wishing to use the PCTE factory obtains an object reference to it. To support the simple applications intending to operate within the context of a single PCTE repository, the PCTE factory supports the operations defined by both the *GenericFactory* and *FactoryFinder* interfaces. The client can then invoke the PCTE factory's `create_object` operation, or pass the factory as the "factory finder" when invoking the `move` or `copy` operations to move or copy within the same PCTE repository. These clients include the servers implementing the `move` and `copy` operations for various PCTE objects as well.

Life cycle creation, copy, and move operations are influenced by a sequence of criteria. Criteria are specified as a sequence of name/value pairs. Certain criteria are of interest to the PCTE factories:

1. PCTE details used here are from the PCTE Abstract Specification, Standard ECMA-149, available from the European Computer Manufacturers Association.

2. As defined in section 5.2.4 of the life cycle specification.

"logical location"

The logical location is used to express the logical connection information that must be specified when creating or copying a PCTE object. Logical location is a sequence of name/value pairs expressing a connection for the object. The PCTE factory supports and requires two:

ORIGIN	A string representation of the reference to the object to which the newly created object is to be connected.
ORIGINLINK	The name of the origin object's link which is to hold the link from the origin object to the newly created object.

"filter"

The filter is used to express the fact that an object being created, copied, or moved should reside on the same volume as some other, nearby, object. A filter is an expression as described in 5B.3. For PCTE, the term "NEAR=" followed by an object reference to the designated nearby object indicates that the new object is to be located at least as near as the same volume to the specified object.

"authorization"

Although omitted from Table 1-4 because no proposal on authorization has yet been accepted by OMG, this life cycle criterion is required to create PCTE objects.

5D.2 Object Creation

The `LifeCycle::GenericFactory::create_object` operation in this specification is borne by factory objects. It has two parameters:

1. a key used to identify the desired object to be created and
2. a set of criteria expressed in an NVP-list.

The corresponding PCTE operation is called OBJECT_CREATE. The parameters to OBJECT_CREATE are obtained from the `LifeCycle::GenericFactory::create_object` parameters.

The PCTE operation OBJECT_CREATE has six parameters:

1. the type of object to be created. This is the "key" from LifeCycle `create_object`.
2. the origin object of the relation anchoring the new object. This is the object identified as the named "ORIGIN" of the logical location criterion.
3. the name of the link from that origin object to the new object. This is the string identified as the named "ORIGINLINK" of the logical location criterion.
4. an optional key for that link. This is the string identified as the named "LINKKEY" of the initialization criteria.

5. an object near whose location the object is to be created. This is the string value of a required filter expression value by the qualifier "NEAR".
6. an access mask. This is the string identified as the named "ACCESS" of the authorization criteria. This string is a simple mapping of the granted and denied access rights.

Exceptions raised by PCTE are mapped to suitable LifeCycle exceptions.

5D.3 Object Deletion

The `LifeCycle::LifeCycleObject::remove` operation in this specification is borne by all life cycle objects. It has no parameters.

The corresponding PCTE operation is called OBJECT_DELETE. The parameters to OBJECT_DELETE are obtained from the object to be deleted using information about that object defined in PCTE's schema information about the object.

The PCTE operation OBJECT_DELETE has two parameters:

1. the origin object of a relation anchoring the object to be deleted and
2. the name of the link from that origin object to the object to be deleted.

To both ensure that the controlling object is actually deleted and maintain the PCTE referential integrity constraints the following steps are performed for each reversible link emanating from the controlling object:

1. Determine the object, o, that the link refers to.
2. Determine the name, r&prime., of the reverse link back from o.
3. Perform PCTE OBJECT_DELETE(o, r&prime.).

The objective is accomplished when all outgoing, reversible links have been dealt with thus, or before that if one of the OBJECT_DELETE calls fails because the object has already been deleted.

Exceptions raised by PCTE are mapped to suitable LifeCycle exceptions.

5D.4 Object Copying

The `LifeCycle::LifeCycleObject::copy` operation in this specification is borne by all life-cycle objects. It has two parameters:

1. a factory-finder to assist in locating a factory that provides resources for the copied object
2. a set of criteria expressed in an NVP-list

The corresponding PCTE operation is called OBJECT_COPY. Some of the parameters to OBJECT_COPY can be obtained directly from the LifeCycle copy parameters. Other required information is obtained from the constraint expression parameter of the LifeCycle copy.

The PCTE operation OBJECT_COPY has six parameters:

1. the object to be copied. This is the bearer object of LifeCycle copy operation.
2. the origin object of the relation anchoring the new object. This is the object identified as the named "ORIGIN" of the logical location criterion.
3. the name of the link from that origin object to the new object. This is the string identified as the named "ORIGINLINK" of the logical location criterion.
4. an optional key for that link. This is the string identified as the named "LINKKEY" of the initialization criteria.
5. an object near whose location the object is to be created. This is the string value of a required filter expression value by the qualifier "NEAR".
6. an access mask. This is the string identified as the named "ACCESS" of the authorization criteria. This string is a simple mapping of the granted and denied access rights.

The semantics of the copy operation corresponds to the PCTE OBJECT_COPY semantics. They are based upon details of the object types involved, including which attributes, links and destination objects are "duplicable."

Exceptions raised by PCTE are mapped to suitable CORBA standard exceptions.

5D.5 Object Moving

The `LifeCycle::LifeCycleObject::move` operation in this specification is borne by all life-cycle objects. It has two parameters:

1. a factory-finder to assist in locating a factory that provide resources for the moved object
2. a set of criteria expressed in an NVP-list

The corresponding PCTE operation is called OBJECT_MOVE. The parameters to OBJECT_MOVE can be obtained directly from the LifeCycle copy parameters or from defaults.

The PCTE operation OBJECT_MOVE has three parameters:

1. the object to be copied. This is the bearer object of LifeCycle move operation.
2. an object near whose location the object is to be created. This is the string value of a required filter expression value by the qualifier "NEAR".

3. scope—whether to move the object itself or the object and all its components

This will be defaulted to ATOMIC.

Persistent Object Service Available Now

No Additional Charge

The Persistent Object Service (POS) is one of the four Services that make up the *Common Object Services Specification, Volume 1* (COSS). The goal of POS is to provide common interfaces to the mechanisms used for retaining and managing the persistent state of objects. POS will be used in conjunction with other Object Services, such as Naming, Relationships, Transactions, Life Cycle, etc. Its primary responsibility is to store the state of the object; other capabilities are provided by the other Services.

The technology adoption process for POS took a bit longer than that of the other three Services and COSS went to press without it. However, POS is now available, for no additional charge, directly from the Object Management Group (OMG). Just fill out the form below and mail or fax this page to OMG, along with a copy of the title page from COSS, and they will mail you the POS addendum.

Name ____________________ Title ____________________

Company ____

Address ____

City ____________ State ____ Zip/Postal Code ________ Country _____

Telephone ____________ Fax ____________ Email ____________

Please return this form, and the title page from COSS, to OMG, 492 Old Connecticut Path, Framingham, MA 01701, or fax it to +1-508-820 4303.